The Smart Interviewer

The Smart Interviewer

Bradford D. Smart, Ph.D.

WILEY

JOHN WILEY & SONS

New York • Chichester • Brisbane • Toronto • Singapore

Library of Congress Cataloging in Publication Data:

Smart, Bradford, D., 1944-
      The smart interviewer / Bradford D. Smart.
          p.   cm.
      Includes bibliographical references.
      ISBN 0-471-51331-8 — ISBN 0-471-51332-6 (pbk.)
      1. Employment interviewing.   I. Title.
      HF5549.5.I6S63 1990
      658.3′1124—dc20   89-37359
                                                                          CIP

Printed in the United States of America

10 9 8 7 6

To my parents,
for their loving guidance
combined with respect for
my independence

Preface

This book is a "how to" course in selection interviewing. It will give a beginner good initial habits; intermediate and advanced interviewers can make vast improvements in their skills. Brad Smart's promise to you is that *if you read the book carefully, and use the "In-Depth Selection Interview Guide" conscientiously, the next selection interview you conduct will be the best interview of your career.*

Self-help books such as those about golf and tennis typically promise *eventual* improvement, given the "unlearning" of bad habits. This book seeks to produce dramatically more revealing interviews *right away*. No muss, no fuss —just a simple, elegantly refined technique that is based on sound psychology and universal management principles.

> ### *No duty the Executive had to perform was so trying as to put the right man in the right place.*
>
> Thomas Jefferson
> 1823 letter to John Adams

> ### *It's a heck of a lot easier to hire the right people to begin with than to try to fix them later....*
>
> Brad Smart

ABOUT THE AUTHOR

In 20 years of specializing in interviewing, Dr. Bradford D. Smart has interviewed more than 4,000 candidates for selection or promotion; trained more than 3,000 hiring managers in how to interview; and improved interviewing approaches for more than 100 organizations. Now the benefits of his training seminars and consultation are yours in this, his latest creation.... the

> ### *In-Depth Selection Interview Guide ... the single most important management tool.*

Smart's first book, *Selection Interviewing: A Management Psychologist's Recommended Approach* (Wiley, 1983), is a widely acclaimed treatise on interviewing. It is a thoughtful, insightful work that fortifies the "links" in the selection chain and significantly upgrades the professionalism of hiring practices.

His premise is simple: Interviewers and interviewees can benefit from much more thoroughness and honesty than commonly occur in interviews. *The Smart Interviewer* is an easy-to-read, sometimes irreverent "guide to the Guide" that is written for hiring managers and human resources professionals. *Smart Interviewing: How to Pass the In-Depth Interview* (Wiley, in press) is a guide for the job candidate. Realizing how comprehensive the interview and reference checks will be, the job hunter can prepare for the opportunity to discuss strengths and reflect on *all* his or her experiences straightforwardly and with an appreciation of the mutual benefits of the process.

The Smart Interviewer elevates interviewing to a new level of professionalism. The approach advocated is simple but not simplistic; due to the author's mastery of the topic, complex principles are made clear and easy to put into practice.

WHAT TO EXPECT FROM THIS BOOK

The Smart Interviewer is an easy-to-use "instruction manual" for the "In-Depth Selection Interview Guide." The Guide, reproduced in its entirety in Appendix A, is reprinted section by section as each chapter in the text explains why the questions are included and how they can be used.

The first chapter illustrates *why* the Guide is so important in light of the high costs—personal, corporate, and national—of "mishires." Chapter 2 details the general logistics of the successful interview, including the all-important "behind the scenes" preparations of job descriptions, person specifications, and so forth. Chapter 3 takes you step by step through each question in the Guide, and Chapter 4 gives practical tips on maintaining the professional rapport that use of the Guide supports. The special techniques of "threat of reference checks (TORCs)" are examined in Chapter 5, and the next chapter details how to put those "threats" into very real and positive action. Chapter 7 delves into the psychology behind replies to interview questions, helping you interpret responses so as to make an accurate hiring decision and aid in developing the hiree. Finally, Chapter 8 looks briefly at some of the legal aspects of interviewing. The appendices present the Guide, all the forms that complement it, and sample person specifications.

What you can expect of yourself as you read this book is the "Aha!" reaction of one whose best instincts are being corroborated and supported. Your confidence in your ability to interview and choose wisely will be boosted, and you will feel truly professional in your interviewing knowledge and techniques.

ACKNOWLEDGMENTS

The author wishes to give special thanks to Sharon Mistele, for conscientiously preparing draft, after draft, after draft of the manuscript; to clients and friends, for critical review and enthusiastic support of the guiding principles of this book, to Don Raden, for his creative cartoons, and to Geoffrey Smart for the cover photographs.

ORDERING INFORMATION

To order additional copies of the "In-Depth Selection Interview Guide," "Application Form," "In-Depth Reference Check Guide," or the "Professional Rapport Rating Form," contact:

> Smart & Associates, Inc.
> 20 N. Wacker Drive #3410
> Chicago, IL 60606
> (312) 726-7820

Contents

The Smart Interviewer

The In-Depth Selection Interview Guide

Of 57,000 managers surveyed in 35 countries, 90 percent list *hiring* among their most important decisions. A decision based on incomplete or wrongly interpreted information can result in a "mishiring"—a situation painful both to the organization and to the individual who has been put into a "no win" situation.

Major corporations estimate the costs of mishires to be two to four times the person's salary. The following list includes even higher estimates, by eight companies, of the costs of hiring a person who quit or was fired one year after being hired, and was 50 percent productive during that year.

COMPANY	POSITION	ANNUAL SALARY	COST OF MISHIRE
Mercer-Meidinger-Hansen	Managing Consultant	$ 50,000	$ 518,000
Johns Hopkins Applied Physics Laboratory	Director	70,000	521,000
Gould	General Manager	200,000	675,000
Inter-Continental Hotels	Hotel General Manager	100,000	529,000
Intelsat	Translator	40,000	162,000
Booz Allen & Hamilton	Partner	250,000	2,000,000
STM	Programmer Analyst	30,000	132,000
EHS	Head Nurse	32,000	66,000
	TOTAL		$4,603,000

With estimates for eight mishires that cost nearly $5 million in a year, it is easy to understand that the annual cost to America of hiring mistakes is $100 *billion* per year. Your reputation as a manager is on the line with each hiring decision you make. You are "playing God" when you hire, and people will suffer if you use your influence unwisely. So, you owe it to yourself, your employer, the person hired, and the nation to be as thorough, professional, sensitive, fair, and objective as you can be.

A key tool in making hiring decisions, of course, is the interview. Research has clearly shown why interviews so often have *not* predicted job

---

***There's something rare, something finer far,
something much more scarce
than ability.
It's the ability to recognize ability.***

Elbert Hubbard
(1856-1915)

---

success, and for two decades, Smart & Associates, Inc. has been devising ways to fix those problems.

The result? THE GUIDE. The "In-Depth Selection Interview Guide" mechanizes and professionalizes the otherwise loose, superficial "art" of interviewing. It is reproduced in Appendix A, and will be referred to throughout this book.

Ninety percent of managers report that the very first time they used the Guide, they got more job-relevant information than ever before. If you are like most Guide users, you will immediately improve your interviewing skills by 50 percent or more by using the carefully selected questions.

The Guide is applicable to all interview situations. Senior executives use it to screen $250,000 division presidents in 4-hour interviews. Grocery store managers use it to interview minimum wage clerks in 30-minute interviews. College recruiters use it to choose future corporate leaders.

Some industry leaders have called the Guide a management panacea, but it really isn't. A totally inexperienced, stupid, or prejudiced interviewer can misuse it. But a capable, well-intentioned user will realize its benefits quickly, especially with study and training. Training, with plenty of risk-free opportunity to practice each part, helps a lot.

The Guide works:

♦ Better than highly "canned" interviews that omit many crucial questions
♦ Better than targeted interviews that ignore how the interviewee developed (i.e., the chronology)
♦ A lot better than the usual "hit and miss" approach in which the interviewer browses through a resumé
♦ A whole lot better than interviews that focus on irrelevancies

Interviewing is not simple. When you interview candidates for selection or promotion, it is not easy to simultaneously:

"I think you'll fit nicely here."

♦ Listen carefully to the response to a question
♦ Wonder if further clarification is necessary
♦ Compose an original question, if needed
♦ Search your memory to see if the current response possibly contradicts a previous response
♦ Maintain enough eye contact
♦ Take appropriate notes
♦ Maintain rapport
♦ Observe nonverbal behavior for clues as to deeper feelings
♦ Tune in to your "gut feelings" to develop intuition anchored in the facts you are getting

The Guide simplifies things quite a bit, however. It:

♦ Provides a clear, logical sequence
♦ Offers correct wording
♦ Has space to write notes
♦ Visually tells you when a question has not been asked
♦ Mechanizes the interview enough that you can look and be professional, and devote your energies to analyzing the candidate

ADVANTAGES OF USING THE GUIDE

The advantages of using the Guide are many. Those that users most often are enthusiastic about are summarized in the following sections.

Ease of Use

The first half of the Guide's questions are chronological, which is so logical that anticipating the next question is easy.

The wording of questions is simple and precise, so that after using the Guide a few times, you will recall the wording to the next question by simply glancing at it.

There is plenty of space to take notes.

You turn the page *after* notes fill the spaces for questions you want answered.

A summary sheet is included at the end for recording conclusions.

Thoroughness

The chronological history tells you how the person developed technical skills, work habits, people skills, motivations. It provides "snapshots" of the interviewee over time, with respect to all specifications for the job. This thorough examination of the interviewee's education and work history is much more valuable than just asking targeted questions about what the candidate is like now.

However, the Guide *does* devote many pages to targeted, or focused, questions. This combination of chronological plus targeted questions is unbeatable.

Flexibility

The Guide is equally useful for interviewing candidates for president or for clerk. The candidate for president is asked for more elaboration on answers to all sections of the Guide. Even in a 30-minute interview for a clerk, sections on high school, work habits, plans and goals for the future, and self-appraisal are asked, though the interview requires less depth of response.

You don't have to change your personality to use the Guide. Extroverts and introverts use it almost equally well. (Introverts do a little better because extroverts sometimes talk too much.)

The Guide is used by most organizations for external selection. It is also used by Fortune 100 companies to assess internal talent, develop managers, help transferred executives get to know their subordinates, and figure out how to smoothly integrate managers of acquired companies.

Legal Acceptability

Forbidden questions are avoided. (Chapter 7 gives further details on the legal aspects of interviewing.)

Professional Image

A natural, warm dialogue evolves as the interviewer smoothly directs the interview, following the logical flow of the Guide.

Thoroughness inspires confidence. Interviewees are impressed!

Learning Opportunity

By retaining your filled-in Guide after a selection interview, you can pull it out six months after a person has been hired to see if your predictions were accurate. If there were "surprises," you can analyze why (chances are, you simply skipped too many questions!).

Succession Planning

In most companies succession planning involves a committee review of performance appraisals, which consist of suspect ratings, a list of a few strengths, and a whitewashed mention of one or two areas for improvement. The committee shrugs its collective shoulders, crosses its fingers and picks the future leaders. The most sophisticated organizations use 10-page assessments based on co-worker opinions and the results of a several-hour interview following (you guessed correctly) the Guide.

Developmental Opportunity

Use of the Guide will produce complete awareness of a candidate's developmental needs. A rich, practical developmental plan can be crafted at the time of hire. Some major corporations use the Guide in the hardest hitting, most effective development of internal managers.

DISADVANTAGES OF USING THE GUIDE

♦ It sometimes takes three or four interviews using the Guide before trained interviewers feel fully confident and professional using it.

Solution: "Practice" on people who are candidates for selection at lower levels.

♦ Without training, it takes 5 to 10 interviews before interviewers feel comfortable with the Guide.

Solution: Get training.

♦ It's more time consuming. Ten-minute interviews become 30-minute sessions. One-hour interviews stretch to 2 hours.

Solution: None needed! Interviewers find it interesting to learn so much more about the candidate. It's also important. After all, if it costs $60,000 to mishire a $20,000-a-year programmer, what's more important than spending an extra hour with a finalist?

EASY STEPS TO SUCCESS WITH THE GUIDE

1. STICK TO THE GUIDE. Ask all the questions, close to verbatim, in the simple, clear, logical order of the Guide.
2. TAKE NOTES—lots of them.
3. REVIEW THE NOTES two or three times.

The following chapters will help you understand the logic and importance of the Guide's questions and techniques for presenting them. With this understanding, you will find it easy to follow the steps to success. And thus you will not incur the personal cost, nor your company (and country) the monetary burden of avoidable mishires!

Using the Guide:
Setting the Stage

When you use the Guide, an interview seems almost to "do itself." However, some consideration of preliminaries and "backstage" preparation will make the interview go even more smoothly and be optimally rewarding. This chapter will give you an idea of how much time to plan on for the interview, how to set the tone for the complete openness you need from the candidate, and how to handle the actual pages of the Guide for best results.

Additionally, the discussion here will familiarize you with the application form that complements the Guide, providing early, efficient, and useful insights into candidates. Finally, this chapter will refine your thinking about *why* you are interviewing—exactly what person specifications the interviewee will be measured against and why they must be developed well before the interview takes place.

HOW MUCH INTERVIEW TIME TO TAKE

The Guide works for 20-minute as well as 6-hour interviews. (That does not include time you need to "sell" the candidate and explain the job.) Most interviews are in the 45-minute to 2-hour range.

The time necessary may seem unusually long for those unaccustomed to using the Guide. Sometimes interviewer trainees ask if certain sections of the Guide should be skipped in the interest of shortening the interview. NO! What section would you eliminate—work habits, technical skills, or self-appraisal? If you skip early jobs, for example, you will miss what is most revealing—how the acorn grew into the oak tree ... how this candidate developed work habits, people skills, and the 40 other qualities that may well include your targeted "person specifications" for the job. So, only skip a section that is clearly inapplicable for the candidate (for example, the Management section for a candidate who has never been a manager).

Following are rough guidelines for the times to allocate to each section of a "Guided" interview:

	45-MINUTE INTERVIEW	2-HOUR INTERVIEW
Opening "Chit-Chat"	2 minutes	2 minutes
Education	3 minutes	6 minutes
Work History	11 minutes	54 minutes
Plans and Goals	4 minutes	8 minutes
Self-Appraisal	3 minutes	10 minutes
Management*	5 minutes	10 minutes
Intellectual Characteristics	3 minutes	6 minutes
Technical Skills*	4 minutes	6 minutes
Personal Characteristics	3 minutes	6 minutes
Work Habits	4 minutes	6 minutes
Interpersonal Skills	3 minutes	6 minutes

*If applicable

The proportion of time devoted to each part of the interview can be "customized," of course, as you develop experience using the Guide and fitting it to the person specifications you are most interested in for a specific position. No one section, however, should be allocated much less than the minutes suggested above for the 45-minute interview, or you will find yourself having to go back to obtain needed information for making your conclusions about the candidate. The longer the interview, the more appropriate is flexible allocation of time.

OPENING MOMENTS

As with any other interviewing technique, when using the Guide, you will take the first few moments to make the interviewee comfortable. Unlike with other approaches, however, you should also take the time to "sell" the candidate on the interview process itself, highlighting the benefits for the interviewee and setting the stage for the frank, revealing answers that you are seeking.

Do the Obvious

Smile, shake hands, offer something to drink, and talk about the weather, parking—something nonthreatening and easy. You are the host and owe the interviewee a couple of minutes to relax.

One interview book suggests unique "ice breakers" such as: "I see you attended school in Belgium. How would you compare U.S. and European educational systems?" Nice ice breaker!

Continue the "chit-chat" opening for only a minute or two, however. As soon as the interviewee has talked enough to exhibit an adequate comfort level, go on to the "unobvious" openers.

"Before we get into the interview, is that enough 'idle chit-chat?'"

Do the Unobvious

After a pause that signals to both parties, "That's enough chit-chat; let's get on with the interview," prepare the candidate for what is to follow. Give an idea of the time frame, and then *sell* the interviewee on being open, honest, and forthright by saying something like:

> *Pat, I appreciate your time today to review your background, interests, and goals to see if there is a good match. If there is a job offered and you accept it, this interview and subsequent reference checks will give me ideas for what I can do to help smooth the transition for you to the new job. Also, by getting to know your strengths and weaker points, I'll be able to work with you better to help you grow and develop. This is a two-way street, incidentally, and after I've interviewed you, I'd like to allow plenty of time for you to interview me—about the job, career opportunities, what I'm like as a manager, and so forth. How does that sound?*

"Great!" is the response most interviewees have to such an opening statement. Instead of anticipating being picked and probed under a microscope, the interviewee can expect real *benefits* from the interview when you are using the Guide.

Of course, a selling point such as your greater ability to help the person grow and develop based on information obtained in the interview should be emphasized only if it is true for *you*. If you will be unusually active in the transition stage for the new hire or have an unusually strong interest in developing new people, by all means say so. If you will not be so involved personally with the person after hiring, the "opening promises" should simply explain that the very thorough approach will help the interviewee and you determine if there is a good match.

GENERAL GUIDELINES

Are you finally ready to ask the first interview question?

Almost. Let's pause briefly to note some guidelines that apply to all sections of the Guide.

<u>Use a notebook.</u> The most useful holder for the Guide is a notebook with a pad of paper on the right and a pocket flap on the left. In the flap you can place the job description, person specifications, and so forth. Place the Guide in the folder on top of the pad of paper and place the folder at an angle that allows you to write comfortably. This lets you take notes unobtrusively; laying the Guide on the desk or table makes it too much the focus. The pad of paper can be used for notes if you run out of room on the Guide. A suitable notebook can be obtained inexpensively in any office supply shop.

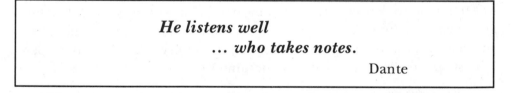

> ### *He listens well*
> ### *... who takes notes.*
> Dante

<u>Scribble notes.</u> Jot down key words conveying the essence of the response. A single response may be significant for a dozen person specifications, and you need a record, so take plenty of notes.

Doesn't note taking hurt rapport? Usually not—note taking with occasional eye contact *helps* rapport because it conveys:

♦ Professionalism (thoroughness)

♦ Positive focus (when taking notes on accomplishments, high points, needs, and so forth)

♦ Sensitivity (allows occasional "breaks" during which the interviewee can collect thoughts, unobtrusively scratch an itch, and so forth)

On each page of the Guide, ask the questions you want answered and skip the rest. <u>Proceed to the next page after a glance tells you that the questions</u>

"When I interview, I don't take notes."

of interest on a page have been answered. It is easy to know when to move on, because that glance before turning a page tells you if there is a question for which you did not jot a few notes.

PREPARING FOR THE INTERVIEW

You will know what questions you want to ask from the Guide because of the preparation you have done in studying the candidate's job application and in making sure that a definitive job description and analysis of desirable person specifications have been developed.

Application Form

The job application reproduced here (and also as Appendix C) complements the Guide and is useful as you plan what questions to ask during the preliminary and in-depth interviews. It elicits basic information that will help you choose among the targeted questions at the end of the Guide.

You will want to study the application form well before the interview and add or delete questions from the Guide according to information there and acquired elsewhere (resumé, preliminary interviews, record checks). Transfer relevant data onto the Guide so that you will be well organized for a smooth running, professional interview.

APPLICATION FORM /
You are not required to furnish any information which is prohibited by federal, state, or local law.

Last Name	First	Middle	Social Security No. ( )
Home Address	City	State	Zip Code	Area Code Telephone ( )
Business Address	City	State	Zip Code	Area Code Telephone

Position applied for_____Earnings Expected $_____

I. BUSINESS EXPERIENCE: (Please start with your present position.)

A. Firm_____Address_____

City_____State_____Zip Code_____Phone (   )_____

Kind of Business_____Employed From_____To_____
                                                    (show months as well as years)

Title _____ Initial Compensation _____ Final Total Compensation _____ Base _____ Bonus _____ Other _____

Nature of Work_____

Supervisory Responsibility _____ Name & Title of Immediate Superior_____

What did you like most about your job?_____

Reasons for leaving or desiring to change_____

What did you least enjoy?_____

Reasons for leaving_____

B. Firm_____Address_____

City_____State_____Zip Code_____Phone (   )_____

Kind of Business_____Employed from_____To_____
                                                    (show months as well as years)

Title _____ Initial Compensation _____ Final Total Compensation _____ Base _____ Bonus _____ Other _____

Nature of Work_____

Supervisory Responsibility _____ Name & Title of Immediate Superior_____

What did you like most about your job?_____

Reasons for leaving or desiring to change_____

What did you least enjoy?_____

Reasons for leaving_____

C. Firm_____Address_____

City_____State_____Zip Code_____Phone (_____)_____

Kind of Business_____Employed From_____To_____
(show months as well as years)

Title _____ Initial Compensation _____ Final Total Compensation _____ (Base _____ Bonus _____ Other _____)

Nature of Work_____

Supervisory Responsibility _____ Name & Title of Immediate Superior _____

What did you like about your job?_____

_____

What did you least enjoy?_____

_____

Reasons for leaving_____

_____

Other Positions Held: a. Company b. City	a. Your Title b. Name of Superior	Date (mo./yr.) a. Began b. Left	Compensation a. Initial b. Final	a. Type of Work b. Reason for Leaving
D. a._____ b._____	a._____ b._____	a.___/___ b.___/___	a._____ b._____	a._____ b._____
E. _____ _____	_____ _____	___/___ ___/___	_____ _____	_____ _____
F. _____ _____	_____ _____	___/___ ___/___	_____ _____	_____ _____
G. _____ _____	_____ _____	___/___ ___/___	_____ _____	_____ _____

Indicate by letter_____any of the above employers you do **not** wish contacted.

II. MILITARY EXPERIENCE:

If in service, indicate: Branch_____Date (mo./yr.) entered_____Date (mo./yr.)discharged_____

Nature of duties_____

Highest rank or grade_____Terminal rank or grade_____

III. EDUCATION   Elementary 6 7 8   High School 1 2 3 4   (circle highest grade completed)   College 1 2 3 4 5 6 7 8

A. HIGH SCHOOL   Name of High School_____Location_____

Dates (mo./yr.) attended_____If graduated, month and year_____

Approximate number in graduating class_____Rank from top_____

Final grade point average_____(A = _____) Scores on SAT_____

Extracurricular activities_____

Offices, honors/awards _____

Part-time and summer work_____

B.   COLLEGE/GRADUATE SCHOOL

Name & Location	From	To	Degree	Major	Grade Point Average	Total Credit Hours	Extracurricular Activities, Honors and Awards
					(A = ___)		
					(A = ___)		
					(A = ___)		

What undergraduate courses did you like most_____Why_____

What undergraduate courses did you like least_____Why_____

How was your education financed_____

Part-time and summer work_____

_____

Other courses, seminars, or studies_____

IV. PHYSICAL DATA:

Date of most recent

Condition of Health:_____physical exam_____

What physical limitations do you have that might have a direct bearing on job performance?_____

_____

List any serious illnesses, operations, accidents or nervous disorders you may have had with approximate dates

_____

V.   ACTIVITIES:

Membership in professional or job-relevant organizations. (You may exclude racial, religious and nationality groups)

_____

Publications, patents, inventions, professional licenses or special honors or awards_____

_____

What qualifications, abilities, and strong points will help you succeed in this job?_____

_____

_____

_____

What are your shortcomings and areas for improvement?_____

_____

_____

_____

VI. AIMS:

What income would you need (in today's dollar value) in order to live the way you would like to live? (Your response will not be taken as dissatisfaction with your present salary, but refers to the salary which you ultimately wish to attain.)

_____

Willing to relocate? Yes_____ No_____ Any restrictions_____

Amount of overnight travel acceptable_____

_____

What are your plans for the future_____

_____

_____

_____

_____

_____

_____

_____

_____

_____

VII. OTHER:

Are you a U.S. citizen? Yes ☐   No ☐

If any personal, financial, or family circumstances might conceivably have bearing on any aspect of job performance, explain in full_____

_____

_____

Have you ever been convicted of a felony? Yes ☐   No ☐

If so, explain_____

_____

_____

I authorize all schools, credit bureaus and law enforcement agencies to supply information concerning my background. I understand that I have a right to request disclosure of the nature, scope, and results of such an inquiry. I understand that if any statement herein is not true, an offer of employment may be withdrawn.

_____
Signature

_____
Date

smart & associates, inc.

CIVIC OPERA BUILDING • 20 NORTH WACKER DRIVE
CHICAGO, ILLINOIS 60606 • 312-726-7820

1987 © Smart & Associates, Inc.

PERSON SPECIFICATIONS

Person specifications are the specific skills, knowledge, characteristics or traits that are defined as necessary for a person's success in a position. The Guide itemizes 44 specifications that can be categorized as intellectual characteristics (for example, analysis skills and strategic planning), personal characteristics (such as independence and adaptability), interpersonal relations skills (likability and assertiveness, for example), leadership/management skills (such as goal setting and removing non-performers), and additional traits (which might be not so much position-specific as company-desirable, such as compatibility of interests with this organization and balance in life).

The first part of Appendix B offers definitions of the 44 items in terms of generally desirable characteristics. The rest of the appendix illustrates how the definitions can be customized for particular positions within a company.

The Cost of Not Having Person Specifications

A major cause of mishires is not knowing what it takes to do the job—the requisite person specifications. Interviewing without person specifications is like fishing without knowing whether you want a

◆ Bonefish (puts up a fierce, challenging fight; tastes like a porcupine, and is not much to mount)

◆ Barracuda (looks mean on the wall, easy to catch, and mediocre to eat)

◆ Bluegill (no challenge to catch, only mountable as a joke, but great to fry up for breakfast)

Companies try to eat porcupines with amazing regularity, because they have not made the effort to define, in behavioral terms, what they are looking for in job candidates.

A major law firm, for example, had been mishiring partners at an average cost of $1 million. The firm had been hiring on the basis of 3 areas: academic performance, appearance, and perseverance (*masochism* would be psychologese for the latter characteristic, since 100-hour work weeks are typical). But some partners who rated high in these 3 areas were eventually fired because they failed to meet 1 or more of the other 39 areas—person specifications—that are among the 44 itemized in the Guide.

Do you wonder how a "sophisticated" law firm could be so shallow as to select against only three person specifications? The truth is, only one out of twenty organizations does much better. The vast majority of companies evaluate candidates on just a few characteristics, such as education, experience, and perhaps "compatibility," when in reality many are crucial for success. Can you imagine a pilot running through one-quarter of the preflight checklist? Or a doctor checking one-third of a patient's diagnostic signs? Yet, most corporations have selection habits that are that inadequate.

Developing Person Specifications

The way to develop the necessary person specifications is to:

1. Analyze the job.
2. Revise the job description (responsibilities, budgets, and so forth).
3. Compose person specification definitions, in behavioral terms, to spell out what it takes to do the job.
4. State a base rating—a *minimum* acceptable rating in order for a person to be offered the job.

Person specifications should not be defined vaguely, but in terms of action and discernible features. Some fairly common person specifications are spelled out in the first part of Appendix B, and these demonstrate the action words and specificity appropriate for defining what is needed in behavioral terms. The rest of the appendix gives variations of these general specifications customized for jobs ranging from president to sales clerk.

"Tell me again. What's so valuable about experience?"

SUMMARY

RATING SCALE: 4 = Excellent, 3 = Good, 2 = Only Fair, 1 = Poor, 0 = Very Poor

Person Specification	Base Rating*	Your Rating	Comments
1. Learning Ability			
2. Analysis Skills			
3. Judgment			
4. Conceptual Skill			
5. Creativity/Innovativeness			
6. Strategic Planning			
7. Pragmatism			
8. Oral Communications			
9. Written Communications			
10. Education			
11. Experience/Knowledge			
12. Motivation/Drive			
13. Initiative; a "Doer"			
14. Excellence Standards			
15. Organization/Planning			
16. Independence			
17. "Track Record"			
18. Emotional Stability			
19. Self-Objectivity			
20. Adaptability			
21. Personal Integrity			
22. First Impression			
23. Enthusiasm			
24. Likability			
25. Empathy/Listening			

*Base Rating is minimally acceptable rating for the person to be hired/promoted.

For most technical or staff positions, approximately 15 person specifications would be the minimum. Any interview for a supervisory or management job, however, should deal with all 44 items. Just ask yourself, which person specification could be eliminated?

Person Specification	Base Rating	Your Rating	Comments
26. Assertiveness			
27. Negotiation Skills			
28. Team Player			
29. Client Need Diagnosis			
30. Political Savvy			
31. Leadership			
32. Recruitment			
33. Training/Development			
34. Goal Setting			
35. Delegation			
36. Monitoring Performance			
37. Performance Feedback			
38. Removing Non-Performers			
39. Team Development			

ADDITIONAL PERSON SPECIFICATIONS

Person Specification	Base Rating	Your Rating	Comments
40. Ambition			
41. Risk-Taking			
42. Compatibility of Interests with this Organization			
43. Health			
44. Balance in Life			

The last two pages of the Guide, which are reproduced here, provide room to summarize your analysis of the interviewee's characteristics. Each specification appropriate to a particular job should be given a *base rating* that shows the minimum rating a successful candidate for that job must have. On a scale of 1 to 4, 4 is "excellent," 3 is "good," 2 is "only fair," and 1 is "poor." Your base ratings should be entered on the last two pages of the Guide prior to the interview. Mark "N/A" for any item not considered necessary for that position. The Technical Professional, Manager Technical Services, Assistant Computer Programmer, and Retail Clerk person specifications in Appendix B provide samples of specification selection and base ratings. The selections and minimum ratings are the responsibility of the hiring manager, with appropriate consultation.

It is advisable that you work closely with a human resources professional to hammer out clear, complete person specifications and reasonable base ratings consistent with the job description, and based on a thorough job analysis. Ask the human resources professional to keep the person specifications on a word processor, so that revisions of job descriptions and specs can be made easily. The samples in Appendix B might form the beginning of these files.

From Preparation to Interview

Having thoroughly analyzed the qualities that are vital to success in the job that you are interviewing a candidate for, and having reviewed the data you have on the individual, you are ready to conduct an interview that will help you make a professional, objective decision that will benefit both your company and the person hired. The data you have entered onto the Guide from the candidate's application form and other sources will assist you in eliciting specific responses. These detailed answers will give you the behavioral knowledge you need to make rating decisions in your post-interview review of the notes you made while listening to the interviewee. Your preparation makes you confident—and the Guide makes it easy. Chapter 3 will familiarize you with the "meat" of the Guide questions and with how important each is to the selection process.

Using the Guide:
Asking the Questions

Now it's time to go "in-depth" in the Selection Interview Guide. You have done your homework, making sure that the job description and the person specifications are well developed and familiarizing yourself with information about the candidate from the job application and other sources. Acting as the cordial, sincere host, you have put the interviewee at ease and sold the candidate on the benefits of a frank, in-depth discussion. Glancing at the Guide, on which you have written in relevant information and crossed out the few questions that might not be applicable, you are ready to begin.

The in-depth interview questions cover education, work history, plans and goals for the future, self-appraisal, management experience and philosophy, and focused questions. As each of these areas is discussed here, the relevant pages of the Guide are reproduced. (The complete Guide is found in Appendix A.)

EDUCATION

The Guide has sections covering high school education, college, and graduate school. The individual's application will tell you how much educational experience there is to cover. But for all applicants, you should ask some questions about the high school experience.

High School

The first questions in the Guide deal with high school. You may not feel comfortable asking about the interviewee's high school days, and that's O.K. Start with the next section chronologically (college, Job 1, or whatever), if you like.

Experienced interviewers *do* ask about high school, however, even if the candidate is 55 years old. Why? To learn *current* attitudes, values, and behavior. When an interviewee says, "I was immature as hell," she is revealing,

---

EDUCATION

So that I can get a good feel for your background—your education, work experience, and the like—let's *briefly* go back to your high school days and come forward chronologically, up to the present. Then we'll talk about your plans and goals for the future.

HIGH SCHOOL

Note to Interviewer: If you are uncomfortable beginning with high school years, skip this section.

1. I see from the Application Form that you attended _____ (high school), graduating in _____ (year). Would you please expand on the Application Form information and give me a **brief rundown** on your high school years . . . particularly events that might have affected later career decisions. I'd be interested in knowing about **work experiences,** what the school was like, what you were like back then, the curriculum, activities, how you did in school, high and low points, and so forth. (Ask the following questions to obtain complete information not included in responses to the general ''smorgasbord'' question.)

2. Give me a feel for what **kind of school** it was (if necessary, specify large/small, rural/urban, cliquish, etc.), and generally, what your high school years were like.

_____
_____
_____
_____
_____

3. What was your **curriculum?** (general, technical, or college preparatory)?

_____

4. What school **activities** did you take part in? (Note activities listed on Application Form.)

_____
_____
_____
_____

5. What sort of **grades** did you receive, what was your class standing and what were your study habits like? (Confirm data on Application Form.)

GPA: _____/_____ (scale)   Class Standing: _____ out of _____

Study Habits _____ SAT Scores _____ ACT Scores _____

6. What **people** or events might have had an influence on your career?

_____
_____
_____
_____

7. Were there any class **offices, awards, honors,** or special achievements during your high school days? (Note Application Form responses.)

_____
_____
_____
_____

---

today, greater maturity. When an interviewee says, "I was a compulsive student then, just as I'm a workaholic now," you get some insights into current work habits.

High school is important in psychological development. Research suggests that most of us devote the rest of our lives to either living up to or living

8. What were **high points** during your high school days?

_____
_____
_____
_____
_____

9. What were **low points**, or **least enjoyable occurences**, during your high school days? (Were you ever suspended, did you ever crack up a car, did you have any serious illnesses?)

_____
_____
_____
_____

10. Give me a feel for any **jobs** you held during high school—the types of jobs, whether they were during the school year or summer, hours worked, and any high or low points associated with them. (If the person did not work during the summer, ask how the summer months were spent.)

_____
_____
_____
_____

11. (TRANSITION QUESTION) What were your **career thoughts** toward the end of high school?

Note: Transition Questions have to do with important choices in life—what to do, when, how to go about it. The answers are often very revealing, not only about the individual at the time those choices were made, but about the person's current attitudes regarding those transition decisions and current values. So, probe very thoroughly whenever major life directions were established or altered.

_____
_____
_____
_____

down our high school image. Ask any teen when his or her most recent emotional crisis occurred and you will hear, "Today." Therefore, do not by-pass a brief discussion of those tumultuous, formative high school years.

To sound professional and to maintain rapport, the opening question you ask about high school stresses job relevance. You ask for:

♦ A *brief* rundown of the high school years
♦ *Particularly* events that might have affected later *career decisions*
♦ *Work experience* during high school

The other "experience" questions about the high school years deal with curriculum, grades, activities, offices, and honors. In general, if the application form shows plenty of successes in high school, the job seeker will not mind discussing those areas. "Feeling" questions induce the applicant to reflect on influential people or events and high points and low points. The reflections may highlight a then/now contrast or illuminate important behavior patterns. Question 10 seeks more detail about high school work experiences, and the last question in this section—"What were your career thoughts toward the end of high school?"—is a transition question.

As noted on the Guide, *transition questions* have to do with important choices in life. The answers are often very revealing, not only about the individual at the time those choices were made, but about the person's current attitudes regarding those transition decisions and current values. So, probe thoroughly when discussing points at which major life decisions were established or altered.

The amount of time spent delving into the candidate's high school years will, of course, depend on the age of the applicant and the educational level ultimately obtained. But perusing the area can provide some interesting insights into a candidate of any age.

College

In general, the questions about college are similar to those about high school, seeking a brief recounting of experiences (curriculum, activities, grades, work experiences or break activities) and reflection on their meaning (high points, low points). Additionally, Question 6 asks about study habits. The answer can be a clue to effort and commitment, procrastination, and so forth. Again, try to get a feel for any work experiences the candidate had during the college years. Question 8 asks about career influences, and, again, you close this area of questioning with a transition question that leads to the next section (either graduate school or work history) and illuminates the person's thinking during a major decision time.

COLLEGE (UNDERGRADUATE)

1. Now about your **undergraduate** days. I notice that you attended _____ (name of college) from _____ until _____ earning a _____ degree. **Why** was that particular school selected? (If more than one school was attended, ask this and subsequent questions about each one.)

_____
_____
_____
_____
_____

2. Would you give me the same sort of **highlights** about those years as you did for high school . . . what you did, how you did, and how you liked it. (Confirm Application Form data. Ask the following questions to obtain complete information not included in answers to the general "smorgasbord" question.)

_____
_____
_____
_____

Question 1 asks why a particular institution was chosen. Responses not only reveal values and decision-making modes back then; what the interviewee conveys *now* is much more important.

---

3. Generally, what were your college years like?
_____
_____

4. What sort of **curriculum** did you focus on? (Follow-up: Exactly what major(s), and why were there any changes in majors?)
_____
_____

5. What sort of campus **activities** did you get involved in? (Follow-up: What was your level of involvement—member, leader, or what?)
_____
_____
_____
_____

6. I see that you earned a _____ (GPA). How would you describe your **study habits** during college? (Look for clues as to amount of effort expended.)
_____
_____
_____

7. Please give me a feel for any **work experiences** you had during college—the types of jobs, whether they were during the school years or summers, hours per week worked, and any high or low points. (If not in campus activities, and there were no work experiences, determine how spare time during the school year and how summer months were spent.)
_____
_____
_____

8. What were important **career influences**?
_____
_____

9. What were **high points** during your undergraduate days?
_____
_____
_____
_____

10. What were **low points,** or **least enjoyable occurrences,** during your undergraduate days?
_____
_____
_____
_____

11. (TRANSITION QUESTION) I see from your Application Form that following college you (attended graduate school, got a job at X company, or whatever). What were your **career thoughts** toward the end of college? What were the options considered?
_____
_____
_____
_____
_____
_____

♦ "Can you believe it—I was good at math, so a high school counselor suggested an engineering school, and I never gave it more thought ... until I found out I hated engineering."

♦ "I was 98 percent hormones and no brains, so I attended the best party school I could find."

Greater maturity now is communicated in reflection on a previous decision.

Comments about THEN reveal truths about NOW

Questions 2 and 3 are general—deliberately vague enough to permit the person to emphasize or de-emphasize, include or exclude information, without being "spoon-fed" question after question. *General questions produce the most revealing responses.*

Graduate School

```
                           GRADUATE SCHOOL

1. _____  2. _____  3. _____
            School                      Date Attended                    Degree

4. Why this school and degree _____
   _____

5. High Points _____
   _____

6. Low Points _____
   _____

7. Career Thoughts _____
   _____
```

The section on graduate school gives you room to note why the applicant chose the particular institution and degree, high points and low points, and career thoughts.

As the interviewee responds, jot notes in the appropriate spaces. When notes have been taken in spaces allotted for the questions you want answered, you know you have at least touched on all of the important topics about the applicant's education. As mentioned in Chapter 2, blank lines on a page alert you to a question not yet dealt with, and no blank lines invite you to move on to the next section.

WORK HISTORY

The work history section is the "guts" of the Guide. Why?

> ### Past behavior is the best predictor of near future behavior.

Sure, it's important to look at the interviewee's education, but for anyone who has had more than a couple years of work experience, the work history section contains the most revealing patterns—how the candidate evolved his or her work habits, work values, management skills, and decision-making style.

There are six work history forms in this section. Each form provides the framework for "all you ever wanted to know" about your candidate in a particular job. If the candidate has had six jobs, you use Work History Forms 1-6. If the candidate has had eight jobs:

♦ Devote five minutes per job for the earliest jobs

♦ Allocate more time for recent jobs

♦ Use a separate pad of paper for jobs 7 or more—or copy a form and change the number. If the person worked for a single employer and had, say, three jobs with that employer, consider each one of those a separate position, and complete a work history form on it.

Why take even five minutes to talk about a job held 15 years ago? For one thing, because *you'll have a deeper understanding of the interviewee,* knowing how he or she has developed intellectual, organizational, interpersonal, and motivational characteristics over the years. Hearing about high and low points, successes and failures throughout a career will enable you to evaluate responses to questions about recent jobs much more accurately.

Frequently, *the interviewee is self-descriptive today,* when talking about incidents years ago.

"Boy was I a hothead then.... Fortunately, if you check my references you'll find I haven't lost my cool in ten years."

"I didn't even know enough to keep a calendar back then—was I disorganized!"

WORK HISTORY FORM 1

1. _____
   Employer   Starting dates (mo./yr.)   Final (mo./yr.)

   Location   Type of business
   Description _____
2. Title _____
3. Salary (Starting) _____ Final _____
4. Expectations _____
   _____
   _____

5. Responsibilities/Accountabilities _____
   _____
   _____

6. Successes/Accomplishments _____
   _____
   _____
   _____
   _____
   _____
   _____

7. Failures/Mistakes _____
   _____

8. Most Enjoyable _____
   _____

9. Least Enjoyable _____
   _____

10. Luck _____
11. Reasons for Leaving _____
    _____
    _____

SUPERVISOR

12. _____
    Supervisor's name   Title

    Where now   Permission to contact?
13. Appraisal of Supervisor
    His/Her Strengths _____
    _____
    His/Her Shortcomings _____
    _____
14. Best guess as to what he/she really felt at that time were your

Strengths	Weaker Points

    Overall Performance _____
    _____

To complete the work history forms, simply:

♦ Ask the questions you want answered

♦ Write notes in the convenient spaces

♦ Go to the next job (work history form) when the page is full—when no more blanks exist next to the questions you want answered.

It took 20 years of diligent effort to develop the work history form—to portray on a single page the road map to get you where you need to go, to permit you to most efficiently use 5 or 45 minutes of interview time you may allocate to discussing a particular job. Professional interviewers, whose careers depend on getting the most job-relevant information in the least amount of time (while maintaining rapport), have given the highest praise to the simple lines and 68 words on the work history form.

How to Pop the Big Work History Question

Let's back up. The work history form is a handy tool partly because of how it is *introduced*. The first question in the work history section of the Guide is a mouthful!

> *Now I would like you to tell me about your work history. There are a lot of things I would like to know about each position. Let me tell you what these things are now, so I won't have to interrupt you so often. We already have some of this information from your Application Form and previous discussions. Of course I need to know the employer, location, dates of employment, your titles, and salary history. I would also be interested in knowing what your expectations were for each job, whether they were met, what major challenges you faced, how they were handled, and what were the most and least enjoyable aspects of each job. I also want to know what you feel were your greatest accomplishments and significant mistakes or disappointments, what each supervisor was like and what you would guess each supervisor really felt were your strengths and weaker points. Finally, I would like to know the circumstances under which you left each position.*

This simple—but *big*—question takes two minutes to ask and essentially tells the interviewee, "Hey, Bub, tell me everything important about your entire career!"

Here's why you should ask that big question:

♦ The typical question/answer, question/answer format is computer-like, dry, and only appropriate when the candidate has a brief career history and is unskilled in interviewing.

♦ By placing the burden of the interview on the interviewee, you learn more. What the interviewee emphasizes or skips over, how responses are organized—*that* is so much more revealing than question/answer, question/answer.

♦ You save time. There are 14 numbered questions, but actually 29, because several questions have sub-questions, and if a candidate has had 10 jobs, that's 10×29, or 290 questions to ask. The *one* big mouthful question can save you a lot of question-asking time!

Do this: Read the full "Now I would like you …" question three or four times and rehearse it a couple of times. Then, use it in an interview and enjoy the benefits. "Try it, you'll like it."

Remaining Work History Questions

Whether you, as an interviewer, spend 5 minutes or 45 minutes discussing a particular job depends on how deeply you want to delve into the questions. For jobs held 15 years ago, the tip of the iceberg may suffice. So you ask the questions, are satisfied with brief responses, continue to build rapport, get brief clarifications, and keep the interview moving along. For more recent jobs, devoting more time to a work history form in order to explore more of the iceberg is justified. Even a cursory 5-minute overview of a job is enough time to dig into detail about at least one specific—an important accomplishment, a crucial learning experience, or a mistake.

<u>Questions 1 through 3</u> on each work history form, seeking basic employer information, job title, and salary, are straightforward, may have been answered on a resumé or application form, and simply clarify the context of the job being discussed. Verify the information and proceed to Question 4.

"A 'minimum security prison' isn't normally considered an 'award or honor.'"

Question 4 ("expectations") is important. Across five or six jobs, the pattern of expectations tells you a lot about the person. Were expectations realistic? Appropriately ambitious? Acquired from thorough analysis of the job opportunities? And are the job hunter's expectations for the position with *your* company realistic and grounded in solid analysis of the company, your style, and the opportunity?

Questions 5 through 9 essentially ask: How did the job work out, what was done, how was it done, and how did the candidate like it? The candidate's own account of successes and failures, pluses and minuses, etcetera, of past positions will present a pattern of attitudes, strengths, and needs that may help you in planning for transition and development should the person be hired, as well as in making the hiring decision itself. It is important to probe the reasons for leaving a job; they may be more complex than as stated on an application form or in a first, perhaps rehearsed reply.

Question 6 on the work history form asks what *results* were achieved in terms of successes and accomplishments. Question 7 asks about failures and mistakes. For every job, at least one accomplishment and one failure should be scrutinized *in depth.* For recent jobs, two or three of each should be thoroughly evaluated. To be balanced, the same thoroughness should apply to mistakes and failures.

Specificity

Dig for specifics! Ask for details of the situation, such as:

♦ Who were key players (individual or shared responsibilities)?

♦ Exactly where and when did it occur?

♦ What were dollar consequences (lost, saved)?

♦ What was the time frame (weeks, years)?

♦ What was the impact on the interviewee's responsibilities and career progress?

♦ What were barriers faced and overcome (or not)?

♦ What were the interviewee's attitudes and underlying values?

Here's another way of looking at how much you need to "dig into" accomplishments/successes or mistakes/failures. Think of levels of specificity as rings on a target, with level three being the outside ring.

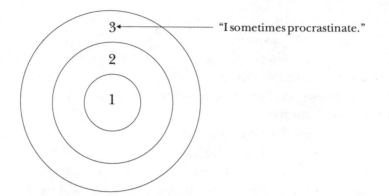

A level three of specificity is so general as to tell you nothing about the candidate. Everyone *sometimes* procrastinates, right? Level two is more specific. With some accomplishments or mistakes you may be satisfied with this moderately specific, but partly vague level of specificity.

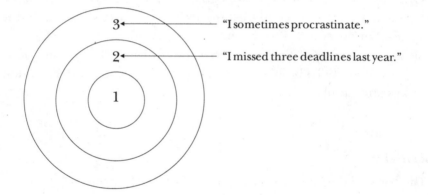

♦ Three out of 3, or 3 out of 100 deadlines?
♦ Your fault, or not?
♦ How late?
♦ What dollar consequences?
♦ What career consequences?

Level one "puts the cork in the bottle." A level one response could have been, "I missed all three of three deadlines; it was all my fault; I got the reports in four to six weeks late; consequently, we lost our best customer; and as a result of that mess I am on probation." With level one responses, you are able to evaluate the candidate, typically on several person specifications. The pattern of successes and failures revealed through a series of level one responses will permit you to rate the interviewee validly on many selection criteria.

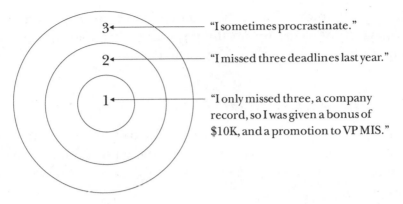

"I sometimes procrastinate."

"I missed three deadlines last year."

"I only missed three, a company record, so I was given a bonus of $10K, and a promotion to VP MIS."

Supervision

Questions 12 through 14, the "Supervisor" section of the work history form, are very revealing. Asking where the supervisor is now and for permission to contact him or her sets up the "threat of reference check" (TORC). (The TORC Technique is so important that all of Chapter 5 is devoted to it.) Getting information for contacting former supervisors suggests clearly to the candidate that reference checks will be done—that any negatives are bound to come out, so it behooves the candidate to be frank now.

Question 13 (appraisal of supervisor) is a beauty! Only a chronological interview guide can provoke such a clear understanding of what sort of person this candidate can and cannot report to. If the candidate has had 10 bosses, the assessments of those 10 bosses say a little about each boss and a lot about the interviewee's needs and expectations for a boss. For example:

♦ A candidate had reported to six individuals, each with a Ph.D. in a technical field, yet each boss was criticized as "stupid," "idiotic," "having poor judgment," "no sense," and the like.

   Conclusion: Just about any boss will be judged as intellectually inferior by this candidate.

♦ Another candidate described 14 supervisors, each with different strengths and shortcomings. In expressing general respect and empathy for all 14, the candidate appeared adaptable—able to "make" relationships with bosses successful.

   Conclusion: A boss does not have to be perfect to win the liking and respect of this candidate.

The final question is a very productive one. It asks the candidate to list his or her strengths, weaker points, and overall performance evaluation *as the former supervisor would have assessed them.* There is quite a bit of space on the form for your notes, because this is an important question. Chapter 5 suggests ways of following up on the responses when the supervisor is contacted. With the past covered, it's time to discuss the future.

PLANS AND GOALS FOR THE FUTURE

The next section of the Guide, "Plans and Goals for the Future," asks the candidate to project or even to dream a bit about possible career paths. Your questioning should tie in with the "Plans for the Future" section on the application form.

Question 1 ("What are you looking for in your next job?") is a warm up. Question 2 may be interpreted as nosy—asking what companies the candidate is considering joining. In fact, a defensive person with poor listening skills may react negatively and reveal a personality "dark side." Actually, the question only asks about *job possibilities*, and most people respond with information about their job interests, opportunities, and locations, appropriately avoiding mention of the companies by name.

"The ideal job would permit me to retire at thirty and provide a nice golden parachute, of course."

PLANS AND GOALS FOR THE FUTURE

1. Let's discuss what you are looking for in your **next job.** (Note ''plans for the future'' section of Application Form.)

_____
_____
_____
_____
_____
_____

2. What are **other job possibilities,** and how do you feel about each one?

_____
_____
_____
_____
_____

3. What about **five** or **ten years** down the road; where do you hope to be by then, career-wise? (Possible follow up: Any wild ideas for jobs that might be fun to consider?)

_____
_____
_____
_____
_____

4. What do you view as **advantages** or possible **disadvantages** of joining us?

Advantages _____
_____
_____
_____
_____

Disadvantages _____
_____
_____
_____
_____

Question 3 ("What about five or ten years down the road; where do you hope to be by then, career-wise?") is ordinary, but the question in parentheses ("Any wild ideas for jobs that might be fun to consider?") adds an unusual and useful twist—it flushes out closet entrepreneurs ("start my own

41

business") and burn-out candidates ("sell bait in the Bahamas"). A little serious discussion of those "wild" ideas can take your conversation to a deep level. This is the moment when candidates often comment, "Gee, I'm telling you a lot more about myself than I intended."

Question 4 (advantages and disadvantages of joining us) is not an unusual question, but because you have reviewed the entire career history *plus* plans and goals for the future, the responses should "fit like a glove." You should now know the candidate very well. At this point you may have included not only whether the person is a viable candidate, but what you could do to change the job a bit to better suit the individual's interests, needs, pluses and minuses. You have many "leads" about the candidate by now; the next section of the Guide can remove remaining mystery.

SELF-APPRAISAL

If you only had five minutes in an airport to interview someone, the self-appraisal section is the section to use. It is largely self-explanatory. To get the most useful responses, introduce this section with a tone of voice that you would use to announce World War III. Slow your words, lower your voice, convey excitement, but speak slowly.

> ### *In the self-appraisal, request an oil portrait, not an instant-developing snapshot.*

The tone as you guide the self-appraisal should be that of your wanting to record the most thorough list of strengths possible. Shortcomings are pursued, but with constant ego protection by you. The attitude communicated is, "I want to fully understand that weaker point, but for positive, developmental reasons." (Methods for delving without destroying are discussed in the next chapter, "Building Professional Rapport.")

The self-appraisal provides you a wonderful opportunity to collect your thoughts, opinions, and feelings about this interviewee vis-à-vis the person specifications. A slow, thorough self-appraisal will permit you to determine just how much time you care to allot to the rest of the interview. It will help you select which focused questions to bypass or include.

SELF APPRAISAL

1. *I would like you to give me a thorough self-appraisal, beginning with what you consider your* **strengths, assets,** *things you* **like about yourself,** *and things you* **do well.**
(Usually it is worthwhile to ask follow-up questions, and to urge the person to continue. For example, you might say such things, as ''Good'', ''Keep going '', ''oh'', nod and ask supplemental questions such as:)

    ''What other strengths come to mind?''

    ''What are some other things you do well?''

    ''What sorts of problems do you seem to handle best?''

Obtain **a list** of strengths and then go back and ask the person to elaborate on what was meant by each strength listed — ''conscientious'', ''hard working'', or whatever.)

2. *OK, let's look at the other side of the ledger for a moment. What would you say are* **shortcomings, weaker points,** *or* **areas in which you hope to improve?** (Be generous in your use of the pregnant pause here. Urge the person to list more shortcomings by saying such things as, ''What else comes to mind?'', ''Keep going, you are doing fine'', or just smile and nod your head and wait. When the person has run out of shortcomings, you might ask supplemental questions such as:)

    ''What personal characteristics do you have that sometimes interfere with the way you work?''

    ''What three things could you do that would most improve your overall effectiveness in the future?''

Obtain as long a list of negatives as you can with minimal interruptions on your part, and then request clarification. (If you interrupt the individual for clarification of one, there might be so much time spent on that one negative that the individual will be very hesitant to acknowledge another one.)

SELF APPRAISAL

STRENGTHS	WEAKER POINTS

MANAGEMENT

The section on management, of course, is used only when appropriate to the candidate's background and the position in question. Though there are only four questions, the importance of the candidate's responses should by no means be underestimated.

The first three questions are warm up. The first, concerning management philosophy and style, reveals how many books the candidate has read on Theory Z, participative management, and how to inspire excellence from sea slugs. The second and third questions (how subordinates feel about you and how you should modify your approach) nudge the interviewee toward self-examination, but are still "typical" interview questions the experienced interviewee will take in stride. The warm up is useful, nonetheless.

Question 4—the request for a detailed description of a *subordinate*—is a gem. It is unexpected, unprepared for, and incredibly evocative.

If you want to know how good a gardener someone is, ask for a thorough description of gardens grown for the past two years, not what the person's "philosophy of gardening" is. The same holds true for management. In describing a subordinate's overall performance, strengths, and shortcomings, your interviewee will tell you more than intended.

"We'll keep you on file, Mr. Moser, but we don't have anything for a 'yes man' right now."

MANAGEMENT

1. How would you describe your **management philosophy** and **style**?

_____
_____
_____

2. What would you suppose your **subordinates** feel are your strengths and shortcomings, from their points of view?

STRENGTHS	SHORTCOMINGS

3. In what ways might you want to **modify** your approach to dealing with subordinates?

_____
_____

4. Would you please give me a **paragraph about each subordinate**, indicating title, length of employment, strengths, short-comings, and overall performance? (Note: Ask this question for *a couple of* positions. Before you leave this section, be sure you have a good feel for how many people were recruited and selected, what approaches were used, how the people were trained and developed, how each worked out in the job, and for those who did not work out well, what happened with them.)

_____
_____
_____
_____
_____
_____
_____
_____
_____
_____
_____
_____
_____
_____
_____
_____
_____
_____
_____
_____
_____
_____
_____

A manager who likes "yes men" will give rave reviews of subordinates who "take direction" and "don't argue with my logic." Those who discriminate against minorities may sound enlightened when talking philosophy, but if actions have excluded minorities, what will your conclusions be?

Instead of asking mushy questions like "How do you train?" "How do you delegate?" or "Are you tough enough to fire someone?" you can judge for yourself as the interviewee describes the subordinates in several jobs. A full description of a subordinate for at least two jobs will tell you a lot about the candidate. Get the full managerial profile in the job—exactly who was inherited, who stayed, who left, and why. Get details of selection, training, and terminations, all through discussing specific subordinates.

Although the Guide recommends a thorough discussion of each subordinate for the most recent *two* jobs, I like to do it for the very first management position, too. Interviewees let their guard down and joke about early managerial mistakes, revealing a lot about current skills, strengths, and weaknesses. The question can be posed as:

> *Pat, that was your baptism under fire in supervision—what challenges and problems did you face and how did you handle them?*

The evolution of values and skills in management disclosed through the description of specifics in the first as well as the most recent two jobs will tell you almost as much as discussions with the actual subordinates themselves.

That is not idle speculation. In counseling with hundreds of executives, I have supplemented the in-depth interview with confidential subordinate interviews. In most cases, the insights gleaned from responses to Question 4 in the management section told the whole story. Subordinate interviews merely filled in the details.

FOCUSED QUESTIONS

After reviewing a person's chronological history, from high school education through every job, plans and goals, self-appraisal, and management, what more could be asked?

Not a lot, necessarily. A very thorough journey through the Guide up to the "Focused Questions" section will equip you with a wealth of insight. Nonetheless, thousands of interviewers we have trained prefer asking at least some of the focused questions, to refine conclusions.

It's like having a matrix approach to interviewing.

The chronology is a comprehensive approach to obtaining most information, and the focused questions "fill in the gaps."

Browsing through the focused questions, you can skip over those where sufficient information has been gathered, and ask those where more insight is needed. This section:

♦ Permits one final, conscious review of each person specification

♦ Confirms conclusions

♦ Adds richness and fullness to your perspective of the candidate

FOCUSED QUESTIONS ON ...	High School	College	Graduate School	Military	Job 1	Job 2	Job 3	Job 4	Job 5	Job 6	Plans and Goals
					CHRONOLOGY						
Management											
Learning Ability											
Analysis Skills											
Judgment											
Initiative											
Planning											
Emotional Stability											
Adaptability											
Empathy											
Negotiation Skills											
Team Player											
Etcetera											

The focused questions have come from trial and error. Thousands of managers offered their favorite targeted questions, and after repeated testing, the ones in the Guide have survived. The questions with an asterisk are *routinely* asked by many managers; the rest are asked only when there is a definite sense that some important data is missing.

FOCUSED QUESTIONS

The following questions for some person specifications are optional. Those with an asterisk (*) are routinely asked. Get specific examples, not general responses.

INTELLECTUAL CHARACTERISTICS

1. LEARNING ABILITY
   a. How would you describe your **learning ability**? In what kinds of situations are you fast or slow to learn? _____
   _____

2. ANALYSIS SKILLS
   *a. How would you describe your **problem analysis** skills? _____

   b. Do people generally regard you as one who diligently pursues every **detail** or do you tend to be more **broad brush**?
   _____
   _____

   c. What **analytic approaches** and tools do you use? _____
   _____

3. JUDGMENT
   *a. How would you describe your **decision-making** approach? Are you decisive and quick, but sometimes too quick, or are you more thorough, but sometimes too slow? Are you intuitive or do you go purely with the facts? Do you involve many or a few people? _____
   _____
   _____

   *b. What are a couple of the **most difficult or challenging** decisions you have made recently? _____
   _____

   *c. What are a couple of the **best** and **worst** decisions you have made in the past year? _____
   _____

   d. What **maxims** do you live by? _____
   _____

4. CONCEPTUAL SKILL
   a. Are you more comfortable dealing with **concrete**, tangible, short term, or more **abstract**, conceptual long term issues? (Please give specifics.) _____
   _____

5. CREATIVITY/INNOVATIVENESS
   *a. How **creative** are you? What are the best examples of your creativity? _____
   _____

6. STRATEGIC PLANNING
   a. Please describe your **experience** in strategic planning. _____
   _____

   b. Where do you **predict** that your (industry/function) is going in the next three years? What is the "conventional wisdom," and what are your own thoughts? _____
   _____

7. PRAGMATISM
   a. Do you consider yourself a more **visionary** or more **pragmagic** thinker . . . and why? _____
   _____

8. ORAL COMMUNICATION
   a. How would you rate yourself in **public speaking**? If we had a video tape of your most recent presentation, what would we see? _____

   *b. How would you describe your role in **meetings**—ones which you have called and those in which you have just been a participant? _____

   c. Describe the last time you put your "**foot in your mouth**". _____

9. WRITTEN COMMUNICATION
   a. How would you describe your **writing style** in comparison with others' styles? _____

   b. Describe your **approach to writing**—do you "write" in your head and dictate a final copy, go through many editing stages, or what? _____

10. EDUCATION (Covered in Education section)

11. EXPERIENCE/KNOWLEDGE (Covered in Work History, although any doubts about level of knowledge should be resolved. Devise your own line of questions to "**calibrate**" the individual's level of expertise. Determine exactly what sorts of **organization climates** (formal/informal, fast-changing/stagnant, growing/declining) the person has worked in and prefers.)

PERSONAL CHARACTERISTICS

12. MOTIVATION/DRIVE
   *a. What **motivates** you? _____
   *b. How many **hours per week** have you worked, on the average, during the past year? _____
   *c. Describe the **pace** at which you work—fast, slow, or moderate—and the circumstances under which it varies.

   d. Who have been your major **career influences,** and why? _____

13. INITIATIVE, A "DOER"
   a. What are examples of circumstances in which you were expected to do a certain thing and, on your own, went beyond the **call of duty**? _____

   b. Are you better at **initiating** a lot of things or hammering out results for fewer things? _____

   c. In what specific ways have you **changed an organization** the most (in terms of direction, results, policies)?

14. EXCELLENCE STANDARDS (Covered in Work History)

15. ORGANIZATION/PLANNING
   *a. How would you describe your **work habits**? _____

   *b. How well **organized** are you; what do you do to be organized and what, if anything, do you feel you ought to do to be better organized? _____

   c. Describe a situation that did **not go as well** as planned. What would you have done differently? _____

16. INDEPENDENCE
    a. How much **supervision** do you want or need? _____
    _____

17. "TRACK RECORD"
    a. What are the most important **lessons** you have learned in your career (get specifics with respect to when, where, what, etc.)? _____
    _____

18. EMOTIONAL STABILITY
    *a. How do you handle yourself under **stress** and pressure? _____
    _____

    *b. Describe yourself in terms of **emotional control**; what sorts of things irritate you the most or get you down?
    _____
    _____

    *c. How many times have you "**lost your cool**" in the past couple of months? _____
    *d. What sort of **mood swings** do you experience—how high are the highs, how low are the lows, and why?
    _____
    _____

    e. Describe a situation in which your emotional **controls** were **inadequate**. _____
    _____

    f. Describe a situation in which you were the **most angry** you have been in years. _____
    _____

    g. What have been the most difficult **criticisms** for you to accept? _____
    _____

19. SELF-OBJECTIVITY
    a. What are your principal **developmental needs** and what are plans to deal with them? _____
    _____

20. ADAPTABILITY
    *a. How have you **changed** during recent years? _____
    _____

    *b. What sorts of **organization changes** have you found easiest and most difficult to accept? _____
    _____

    c. What changes in your **approach** would be most appropriate in your next job? _____
    _____

    d. What actions would you take in the **first week**, should you join our organization? _____
    _____

21. PERSONAL INTEGRITY
    a. Describe a situation or two in which the pressures to **compromise your integrity** were the strongest you have ever felt.
    _____

INTERPERSONAL RELATIONS

22. FIRST IMPRESSION (Evaluated directly by interviewer)

23. ENTHUSIASM
    a. How would you rate yourself (and why) in **enthusiasm** and charisma? _____
    _____

24. LIKABILITY
    a. Tell me about a situation in which you were expected to work with a person you **disliked**. _____
    _____

25. EMPATHY/LISTENING (Determined in other sections of Guide and by direct observation by interviewer)

26. ASSERTIVENESS
    a. How would you describe your level of **assertiveness**? _____ _____
    _____

    *b. Please give a couple of recent specific examples in which you were **highly assertive**—one in which the outcome was favorable and one where it wasn't. _____
    _____
    _____

27. NEGOTIATION SKILLS
    a. Describe situations in which your **negotiation skills** proved effective and ineffective. _____
    _____

    *b. Describe a situation in which you were most effective **selling** an idea or yourself. _____
    _____

28. TEAM PLAYER
    a. What will reference checks disclose to be the common perception among **peers** regarding how much of a **team player** you are? _____
    _____

    b. Describe the most **difficult person** with whom you have had to work. _____
    _____

    c. Tell me about a situation in which you felt **others were wrong** and you were right. _____
    _____

29. CLIENT NEEDS DIAGNOSIS
    a. Describe your methods of **diagnosing client needs**. _____
    _____

30. POLITICAL SAVVY
    *a. How aware are you of **political forces** that may affect your performance? Please give a couple of examples of the most difficult political situations in which you have been involved. _____
    _____

LEADERSHIP/MANAGEMENT

(Questions 31-39 are dealt with in Work History and Management sections.)

ADDITIONAL PERSON SPECIFICATIONS

40. AMBITION (Dealt with in Plans and Goals section)

41. RISK TAKING
    *a. What are the biggest **risks** you have taken in recent years? _____
    _____

42. COMPATIBILITY OF INTERESTS WITH THIS ORGANIZATION
    a. Is there anything we or I can do to **help you** if there is a job change (relocation, housing, schools)?
    _____
    _____

43. HEALTH
    a. Do you have any **health problems** which might interfere with your ability to do the job? _____
    _____

44. BALANCE IN LIFE
    a. How satisfied are you with your **balance in life**—the balance among work, wellness, family, community involvement, professional associations, friendships, hobbies, and interests? _____
    _____

SUMMARY

RATING SCALE: 4 = Excellent, 3 = Good, 2 = Only Fair, 1 = Poor, 0 = Very Poor

Person Specification	Base Rating*	Your Rating	Comments
1. Learning Ability			
2. Analysis Skills			
3. Judgment			
4. Conceptual Skill			
5. Creativity/Innovativeness			
6. Strategic Planning			
7. Pragmatism			
8. Oral Communications			
9. Written Communications			
10. Education			
11. Experience/Knowledge			
12. Motivation/Drive			
13. Initiative; a "Doer"			
14. Excellence Standards			
15. Organization/Planning			
16. Independence			
17. "Track Record"			
18. Emotional Stability			
19. Self-Objectivity			
20. Adaptability			
21. Personal Integrity			
22. First Impression			
23. Enthusiasm			
24. Likability			
25. Empathy/Listening			

*Base Rating is minimally acceptable rating for the person to be hired/promoted.

Person Specification	Base Rating	Your Rating	Comments
26. Assertiveness			
27. Negotiation Skills			
28. Team Player			
29. Client Need Diagnosis			
30. Political Savvy			
31. Leadership			
32. Recruitment			
33. Training/Development			
34. Goal Setting			
35. Delegation			
36. Monitoring Performance			
37. Performance Feedback			
38. Removing Non-Performers			
39. Team Development			

ADDITIONAL PERSON SPECIFICATIONS

	Base Rating	Your Rating	Comments
40. Ambition			
41. Risk-Taking			
42. Compatibility of Interests with this Organization			
43. Health			
44. Balance in Life			

THAT'S IT!

You're done—asking questions in the Guide, that is.

If an interviewee is still "in the ballpark" for consideration, it is natural to switch roles, to let the interviewee ask questions. (Even if the interviewee is by now clearly a non-candidate, a brief question period should be permitted as a matter of courtesy if it was promised in your opening remarks.) Finally, there is the usual wrap-up, scheduling the next meeting.

The important detail of permission to make certain reference calls should be covered. Chapter 6 tells how to make those calls truly productive, even in a litigation-minded society, with people who work for companies forbidding reference-check disclosures.

After the interviewee departs, you're not done with the In-Depth Selection Interview Guide yet. You should:

1. Glance through it, to "see the forest through the trees." Refresh your memory in this perusal.
2. Go through it a second time, jotting down in the Summary a few of the most compelling bits of information for person specifications.
3. Rate the candidate on person specifications.
4. Make one final pass through the entire Guide, to see if all the pieces fit this human jigsaw puzzle.

Oops! What if something is missing, if a few important questions were simply skipped? Or, what if responses, upon reflection, seem to be contradictory? No reason to panic—simply call the interviewee and say you have a few more questions to ask.

Even after the job is filled, the Guide lingers like a magic goose, pumping out golden eggs. Here's how:

♦ *Development of the Interviewee.* You will have the richest, fullest insights into your new employee, so put those to work. Use your Guide to construct a personal development plan. Use the information to smooth the transition of the new employee into the organization.

♦ *Development of You, the Interviewer.* Bring out the Guide after six months, rate the person on the person specifications, and determine where your interview insights were valid or wrong. Chances are, if you "blew it" predicting managerial abilities, you will find that you had not conscientiously asked all the management questions. This sort of self-analysis has benefited thousands of managers.

CHAPTER
4

Building Professional Rapport

The Professional Rapport Rating Form reproduced here and as Appendix E is a handy checklist used in training interviewers. It guides the rating of specific techniques used in initial rapport building, throughout the interview, and in interview probes.

If you have mastered all the techniques listed on the rating form, skip ahead to Chapter 5. Chances are, however, even if you are adept at stroking and smooth-talking interviewees, 25 percent of the techniques are new to you and it would be useful to at least selectively read this chapter.

THE NEED FOR PROFESSIONAL RAPPORT

Why *professional* rapport?

Because "rapport" isn't enough. Webster equates rapport with "harmony" and "agreement"—in other words, being liked. But a selection interview is no love-in. If you are super likable, gushing with perkiness and affability, you might be a sucker, a warm, lovable sap, inviting deviation by the interviewee. After all, most applicants are motivated to put their best foot forward, and not necessarily disclose negatives.

To obtain complete job-relevant knowledge, to be able to rate all person specifications, you should have an interview style that builds liking and, more importantly, *respect*. Both are important. Hence, in the term *professional rapport*, the first word connotes respect and the second word stands for liking.

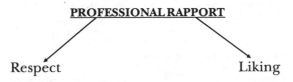

PROFESSIONAL RAPPORT

Respect   Liking

By gradually building liking *and* respect up to, say, an 8 or higher level on a 10-point scale, you will be a friendly professional, in charge of the interview.

PROFESSIONAL RAPPORT RATING FORM

Interviewer _____ Interviewee _____

Observer _____ Date _____

Number of Minutes Observed _____

Rating scale: 4 = Excellent, 3 = Good, 2 = Needs Improvement, 1 = Good Grief,
N/A = Not observed *and* would not have been appropriate or useful in interview.

INITIAL RAPPORT BUILDING   RATING

1. *Greeting* (warm, friendly, smile, handshake)   _____

   Comments: _____

2. Offered something to *drink*   _____

   Comments: _____

3. *"Idle chit chat"* (couple of minutes—enough to get interviewee talking comfortably)   _____

   Comments: _____

4. Stated *purposes* and expected *timing*   _____

   Comments: _____

5. *Mechanics* (appropriate seating, all forms handy, notebook used, private location)   _____

   Comments: _____

THROUGHOUT THE INTERVIEW

1. *All appropriate questions* in Interview Guide asked without harmfully altering the wording   _____
   Open-ended (not yes/no) questions favored

   Comments: _____

2. Interviewer *"connecting"* with interviewee on human level   _____

   Comments: _____

Rating scale: 4 = Excellent, 3 = Good, 2 = Needs Improvement, 1 = Good Grief,
N/A = Not observed *and* would not have been appropriate or useful in interview.

RATING

3. *Eye contact* (minimum of 20%, but no staring) _____

    Comments: _____

4. *Friendliness,* warmth _____

    Comments: _____

5. *Enthusiasm* _____

    Comments: _____

6. *Control* maintained _____

    Comments: _____

7. *Humor* _____

    Comments: _____

8. Appears *sincere* _____

    Comments: _____

9. *Thorough* note-taking on content and context (determined after interview) _____

    Comments: _____

10. *Unobstrusive* note-taking _____

    Comments: _____

11. *Follow-up questions* asked, with appropriate wording and style, and specific meanings determined _____
    for vague responses

    Comments: _____

12. *Absence of* (unintended) *biasing* of question responses _____

    Comments: _____

13. *Interviewee talks 90%* (4), 80%, (3), 70% (2), less than 70% (1) _____

    Comments: _____

14. Appropriate *vocabulary* level _____

    Comments: _____

15. Voice *clarity* _____

    Comments: _____

Rating scale: 4 = Excellent, 3 = Good, 2 = Needs Improvement, 1 = Good Grief,
N/A = Not observed *and* would not have been appropriate or useful in interview.

RATING

16. Vocal *range* (not monotone) _____

    Comments: _____

17. *Expressiveness:* (interested, friendly, half-smile; not blank, not excessive frowning) _____

    Comments: _____

18. Interview *pace* (neither too fast nor too slow) _____

    Comments: _____

19. Use of *applicant's name* (once every 5-10 minutes) _____

    Comments: _____

20. *Show of approval* of openness or when interviewee is obviously proud of an unambiguous accomplishment _____

    Comments: _____

21. *Protection of interviewee's ego* (use of "weasel words" rather than unintended bluntness) _____

    Comments: _____

22. *Control* of shock, dismay, surprise, anger _____

    Comments: _____

23. *Breaks* (every 45 minutes) _____

    Comments: _____

24. Consistently shows *respect* for interviewee _____

    Comments: _____

INTERVIEW PROBES

1. Thorough *summary* (at least one every 10-15 minutes) _____

    Comments: _____

2. Pregnant *pause* _____

    Comments: _____

3. *Affirmation* of understanding ("I see," "uh hu," a nod, etc.) _____

    Comments: _____

Rating scale: 4 = Excellent, 3 = Good, 2 = Needs Improvement, 1 = Good Grief,
N/A = Not observed *and* would not have been appropriate or useful in interview.

RATING

4. *Echo* (repeating all or part of a response)   _____

    Comments: _____

5. *Active listening* (reflecting interviewee's unstated feelings) so as to deepen understanding and profes-   _____
sional rapport

    Comments: _____

6. *Direct question* (usually used when softer approaches have failed)   _____

    Comments: _____

7. *TORC* Methods   _____

    Comments: _____

SUMMARY

Overall level of Professional Rapport achieved

    4 _____

   3.5 _____

    3 _____

   2.5 _____

    2 _____

   1.5 _____

    1 _____

   .5 _____

Think of this challenge as filling two jars, as illustrated below.

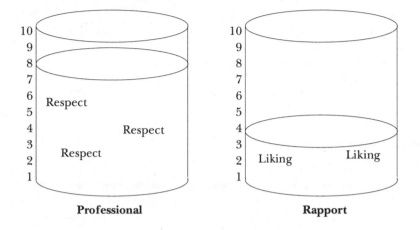

When you have levels of 8 or higher in *both* jars, the interviewee will like and trust you enough to respect your authority when you:

◆ Probe for specifics
◆ Maintain control of the interview
◆ Point out possible contradictions
◆ Require more complete responses
◆ Play "devil's advocate"
◆ Use the TORC technique (Chapter 5) to get the negatives

All these "tough" interviewing techniques can be necessary to determine the candidate's make up and person specifications ratings, and whether a job offer is merited.

COMPONENTS OF BUILDING PROFESSIONAL RAPPORT

Some of the techniques are easy to understand, though perhaps somewhat difficult to execute without training and practice. The remainder of this chapter will comment on all the techniques listed on the Professional Rapport Rating Form, with some concepts receiving more attention than that given the few "self-explanatory" rapport components.

Initial Rapport Building

1. *Greeting.* Your stock (but sincere!) smile and handshake will do fine.

"One more thing.... Do you like hunting?"

2. *Offered something to drink.* Talking causes a dry mouth. So does nervousness. The two together can result in the inability of an interviewee to talk, which is horribly embarrassing. Be sure your interviewee is comfortably hydrated throughout the interview. (P.S. Coffee and pop are fine, but for mellower—Californian?—firms, mineral water or papaya juice are de rigueur....)

3. *"Idle chit-chat."* Five minutes is more than sufficient, unless World War III started yesterday.

4. *Stated purposes and expected timing.* The interviewee should understand the *purposes* (determine if there is a match, facilitate entry to the organization, career development) and *mechanics* (*long* interview, with breaks, but with plenty of opportunity to cite accomplishments, successes, needs). With the ground rules understood, the interviewee will be less tempted to assume this will be another short interview in which taking control could be necessary in order to convey one's strengths.

5. *Mechanics.* Most interview publications recommend seating positions such as

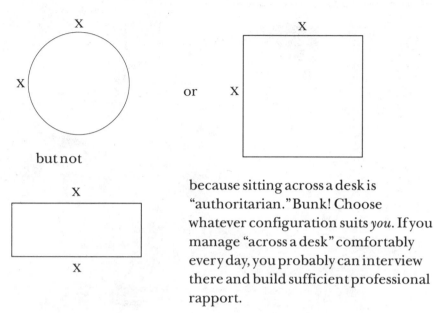

but not

because sitting across a desk is "authoritarian." Bunk! Choose whatever configuration suits *you*. If you manage "across a desk" comfortably every day, you probably can interview there and build sufficient professional rapport.

The location should be private; interruptions insult interviewees and detract from liking and respect.

Throughout the Interview

1. *All appropriate questions in Interview Guide asked.* It's amazing how sticking to the Guide builds rapport. Interviewees *respect* interviewers who ask a lot of pertinent, intelligently worded questions.

2. *"Connecting."* Rigidly sticking to the Guide is not enough, however. Human bonding takes place when spontaneous comments suggest sincere caring and interest, not just professional adherence to a script.

3. *Eye contact.* There should be a minimum of 20 percent (with no staring). That's right—20 percent, not 50 percent, and not 95 percent (as one interview book advocates). All right—for a 20-minute campus interview, 50 percent is more appropriate. But for a one and a half hour interview, the candidate wants a furlough from scrutiny, needs time to fidget or scratch an itch, and respects the interviewer for looking at a notepad while conscientiously writing down strengths, accomplishments, goals.

4. *Friendliness.* You should project at least a modicum of warmth.

5. *Enthusiasm.* There are obvious benefits when you lean forward enthusiastically and inject energy into the interview. Otherwise enthusiastic people are often so conscientious as interviewers, however, that while they are taking notes, anticipating questions, observing body language, and listening carefully—all at once—they happen to don a sour facial expression.

6. *Control maintained.* If the interviewee has read a book or two on "how to out-interview the interviewer," it may be necessary to assert control. Perhaps a power play is not the issue, but your interviewee simply wanders off on tangents or takes forever to answer questions. You need to know if you, as a possible boss, can manage the communications style of a possible future subordinate. The best way to handle domination, avoidance, tangents, or verbosity is to interrupt the interview *early on* and say you need to: get back to the question asked; get a clearer understanding; or speed up, so as to cover all important points. Be friendly, of course, but don't hesitate to assert control, or you will lose crucial respect.

7. *Humor.* If you have a sense of humor, use it to build professional rapport and to tweak out revealing comments.

8. *Appears sincere.* Does that sound cynical? Let's be realistic—an interview requires role playing. You must control shock, dismay, surprise, or anger (see Component 22). While smiling warmly, you may well be formulating a question, or noting body language. We all role play to some extent every day, with our boss, spouse, clients. But it is important in an interview (as in those other circumstances) to be sufficiently *real* while role playing, so that your image is not insincere.

9. *Thorough note taking.* Note taking builds rapport. Yes, a head buried in a note pad *can* be insulting, but interviewees appreciate thorough documentation of successes, accomplishments, goals. Barely legible scratchings are sufficient, and the Guide provides space to make note taking easy.

10. *Unobtrusive note taking.* When mild negatives are stated, you should jot them down, conveying the attitude, "We all make mistakes and have shortcomings and it's good to recognize them." *Major* negatives, however, should be recorded more discreetly.

11. *Follow-up questions.* Ask questions that elicit specificity. You can't rate a person specification such as "Timely Project Completion" if your notes are full of vague statements. Suggestions for achieving specificity were made in Chapter 3.

12. *Absence of (unintended) biasing.* With excellent professional rapport generated, you *may* directly confront the interviewee with a hunch (e.g., "You really don't want a staff job, do you, Charlie?"). This intended biasing of responses is distinct from "leading the witness" unintentionally (e.g., "You're a pretty nice guy, aren't you?"). The latter dilutes respect because it seems, and is, unprofessional.

13. *Interviewee talks 90 percent.* That's right— 90 percent of the time covered by the Guide. Before and after you may talk a lot, answering questions, "selling" the candidate on joining you.

14. *Appropriate vocabulary.* Obviously, the vocabulary level should not insult by being too much above or below that of the interviewee. Jargon and overuse of slang may make the applicant uncomfortable.

15. *Voice clarity.* Don't whisper or mumble!

16. *Vocal range.* Avoid a monotone.

17. *Expressiveness.* Your facial expression should convey enough interest to keep the interviewee talking.

18. *Interview pace.* The pace should be neither too fast nor too slow.

19. *Use of applicant's name.* You should use the interviewee's name once every 5 to 10 minutes. (Sample question wordings throughout this text have illustrated this technique.) Be sure to establish early on the correct pronunciation and what name or nickname the applicant prefers to be called!

20. *Show of approval.* Most interviewing publications say you should be a neutral stimulus, that any positive or negative reaction will "condition" the interviewee to respond accordingly to future questions. That's generally true, but there are exceptions. If you respond with a blank expression and "Oh," when the candidate beams excitedly, "I got the Salesman of the Year Award," the "neutral" response is apt to be perceived as very cold and negative. And, whenever the interviewee takes a chance and trusts you with disclosure of a negative, show appreciation!

21. *Protection of interviewee's ego.* The bigger the ego, the more necessary it is to use "weasel words"—*"could it be,* Pat, that *at times,* you *may be inclined* to delay just *a bit?"* (O.K., this overdoes it.)

22. *Control.* Registering shock, dismay, surprise, or anger could get the interview completely off track. Limit such reactions to sharp (but unobtrusive) note taking. (If a candidate who has expressed an attitude of such repugnance that it automatically eliminates him or her from consideration comes back to you later and wants to know the reason for the non-hiring, you may decide to give the person some feedback on the matter; it is never professional, however, to let yourself be drawn into confrontation with an interviewee.)

23. *Breaks.* There should be a break every 45 minutes, in accordance with what you promised at the beginning of the interview period.

24. *Consistently shows respect for interviewee.* That means 100 percent of the time, no exceptions. You can't earn respect without giving it, and the moment you appear to lack respect for the candidate, the interview might as well be ended. It's much preferable to show respect even if you no longer feel it for the person, and politely end the interview.

Interview Probes

1. *Summary.* This is a powerful professional rapport builder. Summarizing accomplishments or reasons for leaving shows you are paying attention and understand, and it can stimulate additional responses or clarification.

2. *Pregnant pause.* The best conversationalist, you've heard, is the one who keeps his or her mouth closed. Ask a question, and if there is no immediate response, let the silence pressure the candidate for a response.

3. *Affirmation.* Show that you understand with a nod, "I see," "uh huh," etcetera.

4. *Echo.* Repeating all or part of a response shows you are paying attention and can prompt clarification.

5. *Active listening.* The pregnant pause is easy and effective; active listening is powerful and risky. If you sense a person was frustrated as heck, but pretends to have been calmly in control, you may connect by empathetically and sympathetically expressing your hunch in a direct question, as discussed earlier in Component 12. The candidate may conclude you would be a wonderfully sensitive boss.

6. *Direct question.* As already discussed, sometimes a direct question can confirm a hunch.

7. *TORC methods.* Make the threat of reference check real and rewarding. Details are in the next chapter.

USING THE COMPONENTS EFFECTIVELY

How do you keep three dozen "how to's" in mind and use them effectively?

♦ Practice.

♦ Ask someone to observe you and rate you using the Professional Rapport Rating Form. This feedback will ensure your gradually becoming more skillful.

With a high level in liking and respect, professional rapport will add strength and credibility to the TORC technique—the most powerful tool for learning the negatives.

The TORC
Technique

TORC is an acronym for Threat of Reference Check, and it is the most powerful technique available to "get the negatives." Years ago, when writing my first book *(Selection Interviewing: A Management Psychologist's Recommended Approach)*, I reviewed 2000 files of individuals I'd interviewed in-depth, asking myself what clients had received for the fee. The answer popped up quickly—negatives.

Candidates come to interviews well prepared to state accomplishments, strengths, assets, and desires. A full, rich, comprehensive assessment of the interviewee must include failures, disappointments, mistakes, shortcomings, and weaker points. Interviewees may not readily share negative information because:

♦ They want the job—their kids are hungry.
♦ They have defenses, and even if they are motivated to disclose job-relevant negatives, denial, rationalization, and projection may interfere.
♦ Books on job hunting encourage the reader to be less than totally honest.
♦ Outplacement firms do a remarkably good job of training people to put the best foot forward; like political candidates, job hunters are rehearsed, using videotape analysis.
♦ Unskillful interviewers inadvertently invite candidates to avoid negatives by asking too few questions, shying away from questions about failures and mistakes, failing to observe revealing patterns, losing control of the interview and not using the TORC Technique.

TORC WORKS

The TORC Technique works because it convinces the interviewee that:
♦ Extremely thorough record-checking will be done—with all schools attended, some customers, a few subordinates, one or two peers, and, of course, most bosses.

- The record-checking will be done only after the candidate has given permission.
- The interviewer will know so much about successes and failures in each job, that trust, rapport and truth will probably characterize reference calls.

When these truths "sink in," the interviewee concludes, "My only chance of getting the job offer is to accurately guess what co-workers truly have felt have been my strengths and shortcomings." From that point on in the interview, the candidate will reach inside and perform as accurate a self-analysis as courage and insight will allow.

TORC IS APPROPRIATE, LEGITIMATE, AND PROFESSIONAL

Interviewing should not be deadly serious, but the selection process *is*. In 20 years, I have witnessed more mismatch carnage than I care to think about. Square pegs in round holes have resulted in suicides, drug problems, company failures, foolish-appearing hiring managers, and a lower GNP.

The typically silly match-making dance in which interviewers ask the wrong questions about a partial list of person specifications and interviewees come prepared to hype strengths and hide shortcomings is ludicrously shallow, superficial, and harmful—to hiring managers and candidates alike.

Companies have been successfully sued for not reference-checking selection candidates better. Rand Corporation estimates it costs them $225,000 to defend and *win* a wrongful discharge suit in California. Is it not prudent to learn the negatives as well as the positives *before* hiring or promoting someone? Mishires are not just costly to your employer; they make you look bad and cause you headaches—results that are avoidable with proper methods. You, the hiring manager, have every legal right and moral *obligation* to thoroughly investigate the strengths and weaker points of a candidate in relation to all the person specifications. You can look a candidate in the eye and say with pride:

> *I owe it to you, Pat, as well as to my company and myself, to be as professional and thorough as I possibly can in determining if there is a match and, if so, how I can help you succeed. To do that, I need to know as much as possible about your strengths (and anything I can do to maximize those), as well as your weaker points (and anything I can do to manage around them and perhaps help you to minimize or overcome them). By talking candidly and extensively with a lot of your co-workers, I will better understand you and your needs.*

It's Fair

TORC is not just for the protection of you and your company. It's a two-way street. You can honestly tell a candidate:

> *This is not one-sided, either, Pat. Assuming we move ahead in the selection process, I want to provide every opportunity for you to check me and the company out just as thoroughly. In addition to answering your questions, I will invite you to talk with my co-workers at all levels and call people who have left the organization. In other words, we both have a lot at stake—you cannot afford to make a wrong job choice and neither can I, so let's be as thorough as we both can be in the hiring process.*

Though sensible, practical, and effective, this perspective is unusual. The vast majority of hiring managers devote more time and energy to investigating which personal computer to buy than checking out people they hire—the very people who will permit them to succeed or make them fail.

> *Is TORC a sneaky, manipulative technique? NO!*
> *Does it invade privacy? NO!*
> *Can it intimidate? Yes, but this need not be the case.*

"I loved your search letter, and I'd like to hire whoever wrote it"

It's Gentle

In 9 out of 10 interviews, TORC evolves gently. Professional rapport is crucial, and when it is strong the "threat" of reference check is compelling but not intimidating. The interviewee senses that the entire selection process is positive, professional, and thorough. The better candidates welcome the scrutiny; those with something serious to hide are less comfortable.

HOW TORC WORKS

The way TORC works is simple—you just ask questions 12, 13, and 14 for each work history form in the In-Depth Selection Interview Guide. Ask these questions for *every* job the candidate has had in the past decade, and pay attention to the pattern of responses across the person's chronological history. These three questions will reveal not just negatives, but the evolution of strengths and values, too.

Question 12: Identification of Supervisor

Simply asking the name, title, and current location of a former boss implies a check may be done. For jobs in the past ten years, you should ask permission to talk with the boss. TORC is under way.

Question 13: Appraisal of Supervisor

To make accurate judgments of what previous and current bosses have concluded, you must talk with those people, but it is equally important to determine how the interviewee views each boss's strengths and shortcomings. Recently, I interviewed a fellow who described his supervisors as:

> Boss 1: *"A jerk, technically weak."*
> Boss 2: *"Real turkey—a buggy whip, professionally."*
> Boss 3: *"Idiotic."*
> Boss 4: *"Poor judgment."*
> Boss 5: *"Stupid—doesn't read the journals."*
> Boss 6: *"No sense, technically a zero."*

That's six of six, a pattern of negatives which is unmistakable. This candidate can only respect a boss with strong technical expertise.

If you want to know what the candidate needs, wants, and expects from a boss, ask Question 13 for each job. Then ask yourself—can I effectively manage her and, if so, what is the best approach?

With a thorough description of each boss, you will be well equipped to build rapport with each in a reference call. And most important, you will be able to make intelligent judgments about each reference source's opinions of the candidate.

Question 14: Best Guess at Supervisor's Evaluation

What is your best guess as to what he/she really felt at that time were your strengths, weaker points, and overall performance? This is *the* TORC question. Ask it verbatim. Change "best guess" to something else and you'll regret the confusion and loss of time from having to explain that you know the interviewee is not a mind reader. Omit "at that time," and you'll regret hearing that although there may have been problems "back then," the two are great golfing buddies now. Skip "overall performance" and you might conclude that a person who came up with six negatives was a failure when, in fact, the person was considered an outstanding performer (but happened to be self-critical and honest with you).

Again, just ask the questions without apology, take notes, and let the legitimacy and appropriateness of the questions motivate the candidate to respond honestly.

WHEN INTERVIEWEES BALK

Interviewees sometimes balk at the TORC questions, and your job is to smoothly nudge the person toward honest responses. Here are suggestions:

1. Don't ask the TORC questions for jobs 25 years ago or for a job rotation series 15 years ago. Use your judgment, but certainly use TORC for all full-time jobs held in the past decade.

Interviewees balk mostly at the "best guess of supervisor's appraisal" question, particularly the first time it's asked. So, you ask it and then ...

2. Use the "pregnant pause." Your silence will shout, "Please respond."

If the interviewee struggles and truly cannot guess what a boss felt "back then," you should ...

3. Request a self-appraisal—back then. Ask, "O.K., what do *you* feel were your strengths, weaker points, and overall performance *back then?*"

The pregnant pause and self-appraisal—back then work 90 percent of the time.

Occasionally, an interviewee avoids Question 14 by playing games or being manipulative. Maybe there is something serious to hide. Perhaps the person doesn't care what bosses think, or does care and is dense. Maybe a job-hunting book has convinced him or her that any negatives disclosed will kill a job offer. Perhaps the person likes to manipulate, avoid, or control a boss. Perhaps the interviewee is simply not a very direct, truthful person! Or … maybe you haven't figured out why TORC is avoided.

You owe it to yourself, the candidate, and your organization to not fail in this "moment of truth." Without solid, compelling answers to the important TORC question, you probably will not extend a job offer. What a shame, if the candidate is excellent and for some reason is uncharacteristically inclined to play games with you at this moment. You must *sell* the candidate on the benefits of responding well. If the interviewee guesses what a boss felt strengths but omits negatives, all that is usually necessary is repeating, "and what did he feel were your weaker points?" Don't be rude, don't show irritation—just do your professional best. Here's how:

- *Avoider:* "You'll have to call her to find out what she thought of my performance."

  You: "I'll do that, John, but I'm interested in your insights into an important relationship—with your boss. I don't expect you to read her mind, but do try to guess what she felt were your strengths, weaker points, and overall performance back then."

- *Avoider:* "The performance appraisal system wasn't good, so I don't know what he felt were my shortcomings."

  You: "Performance appraisal systems usually aren't good, so just do your best and guess."

- *Avoider:* "My boss was ill that year and hardly communicated with anyone."

  You: "OK … what would *you* say were your shortcomings in that job?"

- *Avoider:* "Why are you so interested in what my bosses have felt about me?"

  You: "That's a fair question, Susan. I'll tell you why. In the first place, people have succeeded here if they have been interested in how I feel about their performance. Being interested is not enough, however, since you can be interested but not very perceptive. I like it when subordinates *are* perceptive—when they take hints. Finally, it's a good sign if at this third meeting, you show enough trust in me and my judgment to disclose not just positives, but realistic negatives."

By pressing a bit, you nudge the avoider to think, "Good grief, this interviewer is going to thoroughly record-check me and get former co-workers to tell him my strengths *and shortcomings*. If I can't guess what bosses and others will say, I won't get the job, because this guy will conclude I'm unconcerned with what bosses think, I do care but I'm dense, I don't trust him yet ... or all of the above!"

You get the picture. There are hundreds of avoidance ploys and dozens of ways to counteract them. The important thing is to gently persist in encouraging thoughtful, truthful responses to Question 14. You'll be amazed at your success: Interviewees get the message, comply, and provide the additional data to permit you to make an informed hiring decision.

TORC AND THE CURRENT EMPLOYER

A job offer should be contingent upon "no surprises" in reference checks with the current employer. Naturally, a candidate might prohibit checks until an offer is accepted, and, naturally, you will respect that. When you get to Question 14 for the current job, say:

> *Pete, if an offer is made in writing and you formally accept, I'll naturally want to talk with Sam, your boss. Now, don't worry—no offer has ever, to my knowledge, been withdrawn because of a current employer check. But in talking with a current boss, I frequently get an additional insight or suggestion that can help a new employee succeed.*

Then re-ask Question 14!

TORC IS NO BLUFF

TORC is a threat, but no bluff. You should conduct thorough reference checks, and by comparing those with responses to Question 14, see a pattern across person specifications and job history that paints a vivid picture of the candidate. Bosses should be contacted, but in reviewing job history, you may conclude certain peers, subordinates, or customers would be valuable sources, too. Fine—call them, with permission.

In fact, it is very useful to enlist the candidate's cooperation in setting up reference calls. When confirming the name, title, and location of a supervisor whom you will probably want to call for a reference, ask the candidate, "Would you please contact (the previous supervisor) at home, and ask if she would accept a telephone call from me at home sometime soon?" This is important. In that simple sentence you ask the candidate to do the legwork *and* inspire more honest interview responses because the inevitability of thorough reference calls is driven home.

A potential disadvantage is that your candidate will use the call to a former boss to influence what that boss will say. Judge for yourself if your candidate seems to be a "straight shooter." The risk is apt to be minor. For a glib game player, however, you may wish to make the reference calls without the candidate "running interference."

The next chapter will give you detailed suggestions for making productive reference calls. These calls will logically follow up on responses to interview questions, especially those involving self-appraisal. They may help you crystallize your selection decision, and you may receive additional ideas about how best to integrate the selectee's working patterns into your organization to the mutual benefit of all.

CHAPTER

6

Conducting
Productive
Reference Calls

Since TORC is no bluff, reference calls are always made. But will reference calls be accepted? If you follow the guidelines of this chapter, most reference calls you conduct *will* give you valuable insights into your selection candidate, despite the fact that most major companies prohibit managers from disclosing reference information.

REFERENCE-CHECK BARRIERS

Picture Charlie, the job seeker, who was fired from Acmeworld Enterprises because he just could not learn enough about robotics to run a machine efficiently. Charlie was slow, made mistakes, and failed the robotics course three times. Charlie, incidentally, has a wife and five children who like to eat three meals a day. Suppose prospective employers called Charlie's bosses and heard:

- "Charlie ... Yeah, nice guy, but stupid. I wouldn't hire him."
- "Oh, yeah, Charlie ... Just didn't try hard. Kinda lazy, I think."

Suppose Charlie sued Acmeworld Enterprises. Picture a jury listening to testimony in which a mega-powerful company appears to assassinate the character of poor Charlie, leaving him unable to get a job, unable to feed his children. Picture how fat that award to Charlie could be.

Of course, Acmeworld and almost all large companies have policies that prevent such pictures from developing. So, if you, the hiring manager, want to check Charlie's references, then you probably will be required to get Charlie's written permission, permitted to talk with the Human Resources department of Charlie's former employers, and given little more than confirmation of dates of employment and job title. Charlie's former bosses have no doubt been instructed to comply with policies that say, "Do not accept reference-check calls."

SO WHY BOTHER?

So why should you bother to make reference-check calls in the face of such resistance? Because the barriers are not insurmountable. Hiring managers report that much to their amazement 80 percent of the reference sources they seek out *do* talk to them—when they follow the guidelines stated in this chapter. Those references are trusting that people like you will not permit criticism of your candidate to cause them embarrassment or get them into trouble.

Are you worthy of that trust? Are you uncomfortable asking a person to violate company policy? Isn't it a shame that in this litigation-minded society there are people we can talk with who can help us get round pegs into round holes and avoid mishires, and yet companies are understandably hesitant to give valuable, job-relevant insights.

Actually, the situation is worse than described. Courts are increasingly finding companies like yours *liable* for hiring bad guys (rapists, for example) because your company failed to perform record checks! (For you legal eagles, see *Milorney v. B&L, Sheerin v. Holis, Cramer v. Housing Opportunities Committee*). How's that for a catch 22? It's prudent for companies to withhold information on former employees, but companies are vulnerable to litigation if they don't check prospective employees' records.

Candidate records can be obtained from schools, credit bureaus, and court records; the legal protection for sources and candidates is appropriately solid. The real barriers exist for reference discussions with former co-workers and bosses. But, fortunately, these barriers are surmountable for several reasons.

A main breach in the reference wall is that sources (usually former bosses) feel it is *moral* and *right* to give their opinion on former employees. Policies prohibiting managers from talking with prospective employers like you are vaguely written, thus making noncompliance less threatening. "Reference check" is rarely defined in company policies, let alone in standard dictionaries (yet). I have never seen a policy specifically forbidding taking a *personal call* regarding a former employee *at home*, which is exactly what this chapter suggests you request of a reference.

Companies like yours can be very tight about information *released* on former employees, yet encourage hiring managers like you to make a *personal call* to a candidate's former co-workers. Naturally, such personal calls will not go in personnel files. The image of company hypocrisy is avoided because your Human Resources department can give out only minimal information and, when performing "reference checks," contacts other H.R. departments and requests only the same name, rank, and serial number.

In other words, hiring managers like you are getting around other companies' reference restrictions by making personal calls to former co-workers with whom you want to talk. That's the basic premise, although details of the "In-Depth Reference Check Guide" are important, to improve the chances that reference calls will produce valuable insights.

PRINCIPLES OF MAKING REFERENCE CALLS

The basic principles that make reference calls productive are stated in 10 bulleted points on page 1 of the "In-Depth Reference Check Guide," which is elaborated upon here and can also be found in Appendix D.

♦ In-depth reference checks should be conducted by the hiring manager. (Human Resources should conduct preliminary reference checks, early in the selection process, simply to verify dates of employment and job title).

Early in the selection process, the Personnel Clerk, Pat, should routinely conduct preliminary checks, merely to confirm basic facts. Pat probably has not even met the candidate, so any attempt to contact former bosses would be a waste of time. Those bosses would sense Pat is performing a routine clerical function, and either refer Pat to their Human Resources department or give "whitewash" comments.

When you, the hiring manager, call previous bosses, the "flavor" is elevated. Your title, composure, and clear seriousness of purpose earn you credibility, respect, and trust. You are a colleague, not a clerk.

♦ In-depth reference checks should be performed *after* the in-depth selection interview.

After the in-depth selection interview, you will know more about the candidate in some important respects than do the previous bosses you call. That's right, and that is *usually* the situation. Your in-depth knowledge of the candidate magnifies your credibility.

As soon as the reference says, "Sam was pretty well organized," you may interrupt and pleasantly say, "I'll bet you wouldn't say Sam was *very* well organized. Sam admitted to me that he was four months late on the San Diego project because he had not checked delivery times. He also told me he trusts his memory too much and doesn't have 'to-do' lists or tickler files." That will end any "whitewash" attempt.

During the in-depth interview, you got Sam's assessment of his boss, which helps you position yourself and your questions. Even before calling the former boss, you have a good idea whether that person is competent, open, political, friendly, or whatever, and that knowledge gives you more power in your reference call.

Of course, if you have a network of trusted sources you can call for the "straight scoop" on a candidate, it is appropriate to call *before* the in-depth selection interview. The point is that there are significant barriers to getting honest, complete reference information, but the in-depth selection interview gives you added psychological leverage when talking with references.

♦ Contact previous supervisors, particularly those the applicant has reported to during the past five years.

But don't limit yourself too much. During the interview you may decide that an influential peer or a talented subordinate or perhaps a particularly demanding customer would be worth talking to. Previous bosses were primarily responsible for directing your candidate, however, so they are apt to represent 80 percent of the folks with whom you would like to talk.

♦ Obtain written permission from the applicant to conduct reference checks.

The application form (Appendix C) has a written authorization statement, with signature required, at the bottom of the last page. Just below Job G on the second page is:

> *Indicate by letter* _____ *any of the above employers you do* not *wish contacted.*

Some companies go a bit further and have the candidate sign a special authorization form for each person to be contacted.

♦ Do not call those listed as "references" in a resumé … unless the list contains a recent supervisor's name.

The references listed in a resumé sometimes include the candidate's brother-in-law, insurance agent, and priest. When the candidate includes former bosses, that fact is a plus, for it suggests that there is nothing to hide.

♦ During the in-depth selection interview, ask the applicant the name, title, and location of each supervisor. Then ask the applicant, "Would you please contact (the previous supervisor) at home, and ask if she would accept a telephone call from me at home sometime soon?"

This preparation step was discussed in the previous chapter.

♦ Promise those contacted total confidentiality, and honor that promise.

It is very important to consider the situation of the person you are contacting. To be completely fair with the reference source, you might say, "Your company probably restricts reference calls, and I'll understand if you cannot talk with me." If *your* company considers this a personal call, with no records kept and with you being morally obligated to maintain confidentiality, say that too.

♦ Contact the person at home, preferably on the weekend.

If the candidate initially contacts the references you choose, subsequent calls by you at the reference's home can usually be arranged. Reference sources generally are more relaxed and willing to take time to talk outside the office.

♦ Create the tone in which you are a trusted colleague … a fellow professional who knows the applicant very well, who just might hire the applicant, and who is apt to better manage the applicant if the person contacted will be kind enough to share some insights.

You are not a personnel clerk conducting a routine reference check. When you immediately elevate the tone with a source who has already agreed to talk with you, trust is inspired.

♦ Contact the current supervisor. If this is not acceptable to the applicant until a written offer is formally accepted, make it clear that a job offer will be contingent upon "no surprises" in reference checks that will be performed at a mutually agreed upon time.

In Chapter 5, suggested TORC wording was offered. By emphasizing how a discussion with the current boss could help the candidate in the next job, TORC operates at its positive, legitimate best.

If the candidate is insightful and honest, there will be no surprises from the current boss. And, current bosses often *do* offer a good suggestion for fitting a mostly round peg into a mostly round hole.

REFERENCE-CHECK COMPONENTS

The remaining sections of the "In-Depth Reference Check Guide" are:

♦ Suggested introduction comments
♦ Comprehensive appraisal of the candidate
♦ Responsibilities/Accountabilities
♦ Overall performance rating

- ◆ Confirmation of dates/compensation
- ◆ Description of position applied for
- ◆ Good/Bad fit appraisal
- ◆ Comprehensive ratings
- ◆ Questions for me as hiring manager
- ◆ Final comments
- ◆ Thanks!…with double check on confidentiality expectations

If you comport yourself professionally, the chances are good that the source will say, "I'll trust your judgment as to who should know what my opinions of Chris are." If the person holds you to strict confidentiality and wants his or her comments shared with no one, keep your promise!

While following the chronological order in the "In-Depth Selection Interview Guide" is important, filling in all the sections of the "In-Depth Reference Check Guide" may not be necessary. A thorough discussion of the candidate will probably hit on most or all of the sections of the Reference Guide, but since most references have shallower insights into your candidate than you, eventually the reference comments become redundant, and it's time to say thanks and close.

REFERENCE-CHECK RESULTS

Having enumerated the awesome barriers to getting useful reference comments and having described ways that companies use to appropriately circumvent those barriers, we have a final comment that may surprise you:

> *Candid reference opinions*
> *seldom add crucial insights.*

That's right—even when former bosses, customers, peers, and subordinates share their most honest opinions about your candidate, you will generally conclude, "I really didn't learn anything to change the conclusions I reached upon completion of the in-depth selection interview."

Even so, the feeling of confirmation is very satisfying, and it is worth your time to make the calls. By noticing nuances and subtle distinctions, by getting a few suggestions for how to best manage the person, you can feel confident that no stone has been unturned in an effort to fully understand the people you hire.

Introductory Comments

"Hello, (name of person contacted), thank you very much for (returning/accepting) my call. As (A) indicated, we are considering hiring him and I would **very much** appreciate your comments on his strengths, areas for improvement and how I might best manage him. Could I impose on you for a few minutes to get your insights -- it would be very helpful to (A) and me. And, of course, anything you tell me will be held in the strictest confidence." (Assuming concurrence ...) "Great, thank you very much. (A) and I have spent _____ hours together... I have thoroughly reviewed his career history and plans for the future and I was particularly interested in his experiences when he reported to you. If you don't mind, why don't we start with a very general question ..."

Comprehensive Appraisal

"What would you consider (A)'s:

Strengths, Assets, Things You Like and Respect About Him, Personally and Professionally, and His ...	Shortcomings, Weaker Points, and Areas For Improvement?"

Notes:

- It is OK to interrupt strengths to get clarification, but do not do so for shortcomings. Get the longest list of shortcomings possible and then go back for clarification. If you interrupt the negatives and get elaboration, the tone might seem too negative, thus closing off discussion of further negatives.

- If you are getting a "white wash," inquire about negatives directly. For example: "John said that he missed the software project due date by three months and guesses that that hurt his overall performance rating. Could you elaborate?"

Responsibilities/Accountabilities

"Would you please clarify what (A)'s responsibilities and accountabilities were in that position?"

_____

_____

_____

Overall Performance Rating

"On a scale of excellent, good, fair or poor, how would you rate (A)'s overall performance?

_____

Why? _____

Is (A) eligible for re-hire?" _____

Confirmation of Dates/Compensation

"Just to clean up a couple of details, what were (A)'s starting _____
and final _____ employment dates? What were his initial _____
and final _____ compensation levels?"

Description of Position Applied For

"Let me tell you more about the job (A) is applying for." (Describe the job)

Good/Bad Fit

"Now, how do you think (A) might fit in that job?" (Probe for specifics)

Good Fit Indicators	Bad Fit Indicators

Comprehensive Ratings

"Now that I've described the job that (A) is applying for and you've told me quite a bit about his strengths and shortcomings, would you please rate him on nine categories? An excellent, good, fair, and poor scale would be fine."

	Rating	Comments *
1. Thinking skills ... judgement, analytic ability, pragmatism, decisiveness, creativity, ability to juggle several projects simultaneously		
2. Communications ... one-one, in meetings, speeches, and written communications		
3. Technical skills/experience/ education		
4. Initiative, perseverance, independence, high standards of performance		
5. Emotional stability and maturity, willingness to admit mistakes and absence of personal problems that might interfere with the job		
6. Work habits ... time management, organization and planning		
7. People skills ... first impression made, ability to win the liking and respect of people, assertiveness, cooperativeness, willingness to take direction, enthusiasm and empathy		
8. Motivation/drive/ambition/health		
9. Managerial abilities ... leadership, ability to hire the best people, ability to train and develop people, willingness to fire those who are hopelessly incompetent, delegation, monitoring performance and creating team efforts		

* **Note:** Probe for specifics. Don't accept vague generalities ("he sometimes procrastinates") but ask for concrete examples, dates, consequences, etc.

Questions for Me as Hiring Manager
"What would be your best advice to me for how I could best manage (A)?"

_____

_____

_____

_____

_____

_____

Final Comments
"Have you any final comments or suggestions about (A)?"

_____

_____

_____

_____

_____

_____

Thanks!
"I would like to thank you very much for your insightful and useful comments and suggestions. Before we close, please let me know which of your comments I can share with others and which should be just between the two of us."

_____

_____

_____

_____

_____

_____

smart & associates, inc.

CIVIC OPERA BUILDING • 20 NORTH WACKER DRIVE
CHICAGO, ILLINOIS 60606 • 312-726-7820

How to Interpret Responses

The question of how to interpret responses, phrased differently, is, how can the interviewer arrive at valid ratings on all person specifications, drawing from:

♦ Resumé analysis
♦ Application form analysis
♦ Preliminary interviews
♦ In-Depth selection interview
♦ Co-worker interviews
♦ Reference checks
♦ Casual interactions

Interpretation advice given here has evolved from training interviewers—thousands of them, including senior human resource professionals, search executives, and management psychologists. The method involves case studies, in-depth interviews videotaped and analyzed thoroughly. Trainees are called upon to:

♦ Rate the interviewee on all person specifications
♦ Justify the ratings with specific and compelling data from the interview
♦ Defend the ratings and supportive data among peers

In a two-day workshop, trainees learn that interpretations of responses must either be airtight, or additional questions should be asked. In other words:

> **There is no excuse for unsubstantiated "hunches."**

When all available data have been gathered, even experienced interviewers rely on certain principles to guide interpretation.

The following advice[1] has proven useful to interviewers of CEOs, vice-presidents, managers, professionals, clerks, and hourly workers.

1. ADHERE TO THE BASICS

Valid interpretation can only come from thorough, accurate data. "Garbage-in, garbage-out" applies equally to computer and interview interpretation. The basics include:

♦ Conducting a thorough *job analysis* (do you understand the job?)

♦ Writing broad, behaviorally anchored *person specifications* (do you know the standards against which candidates should be measured?)

♦ Conducting an *in-depth selection interview* (did you ask all the questions you should have in the Guide?)

♦ Operating *within the law* (stick with the Guide—EEO loves job-relevant questions, thorough notes, and behaviorally anchored person specifications)

♦ Taking *thorough notes* (rather than relying on your memory)

♦ *Reviewing interview notes* three times (rather than trusting a gut feel at the end of the interview)

♦ Trying to *control prejudices and stereotypes* (by incorporating opinions of co-workers who conducted brief interviews)

♦ Avoiding *unintended biasing* responses (by using wording in the Guide and, when asking for clarification or devising an original question, using open-ended rather than yes-no questions, and not "leading the witness")

♦ Retaining *control* of the interview (rather than losing control, which can only result in insufficient data for ratings and probably no job offer)

♦ Achieving *specificity* (rather than accepting vague responses)

All right, suppose you have performed the mechanics—you have all the data a skilled interviewer would need in order to arrive at valid interpretation. What next?

---

[1] Some of this advice is excerpted from Bradford Smart, *Selection Interviewing: A Management Psychologist's Recommended Approach,* John Wiley & Sons, 1983.

2. LOOK FOR PATTERNS

A sea slug can accurately interpret patterns … on the sea floor. Response patterns in interviews are a hiring manager's Rosetta stone—by far the most valuable resource for interpretation. Patterns are incredibly useful and can only result from an *in-depth selection interview*, incorporating *chronological review* in which at least a dozen questions are asked about every job, followed by specific, *targeted questions* on person specifications.

Permit me to digress, to make a point. Interviewing books generally recommend specific, targeted questions vis-à-vis a few (not all) crucial person specifications and suggest either no chronological review or only a cursory one. How insufficient!

As an example of such a flawed approach, let's consider how to rate a person's organization skills. An interviewer might ask for specific examples of how the interviewee's organization skills have succeeded and have failed. Responses in a real case study (Jan, a brand manager in a manufacturing company) were:

♦ "I was most organized last August on the United Way drive—contacted everyone in our company, followed up twice as required, and we met the goal. I presented a full report on time and the CEO said, 'Jan, you are super organized.'"

♦ "I was most disorganized when six months pregnant. I forgot things, lacked energy to follow up, and, I'll admit it, I dropped the ball."

Can you rate Jan on her organization habits? If there were 18 person specifications, and you elicited specifics of the single best and worst occurrences, the interview could last 90 minutes … and *then*, could you rate Jan?

I could not. I've tried, observed experts in this approach, and inevitably concluded that the data are like Swiss cheese—full of holes.

People say, "Oh, it's easy for you to interpret responses because you have a Ph.D. in psychology, 20 years of experience, and 4000 in-depth interviews under your belt." And I say, take away the chronological portion of the interview and leave me only with specific, targeted questions to ask, and I'll be less perceptive than a sea slug.

The chronological portion of an interview with Jan would have produced these insights:

♦ High School—successfully juggled academics (B average), sports (captain of girls' field hockey team), leadership (chairperson of Prom Committee), and 20 hours of work per week during school year (accounting clerk).

♦ Job 1—enjoyed organizing three marketing analyst projects simultaneously. Promoted. Boss complimented her on tying up all loose ends where others had failed.

♦ Job 2—initiated a system, using PC, to chart progress on projects. Boss rated her "exceptional" and she guesses he would list among her strengths, "compulsive detail person."

You get the point. In jobs 3, 4, and 5, Jan was also superbly organized. On top of that, her application form was impeccable and her answers to questions well thought out. After one and a half hours in a chronological interview, the specific, targeted questions were asked, the responses concerning United Way and pregnancy problems elicited, and the interpretation became clear: She is, today, a superbly organized person and only extraordinary circumstances would render her less so.

Patterns—across high school, college, six or eight jobs—prepare you to "fine tune" your calibration of a candidate in the latter half of the interview, using the specific, targeted questions. As you probe for specifics across that chronological history, single examples and incidents often simultaneously reveal insights into four or five person specifications. The candidate's intellectual, interpersonal, administrative, and motivational characteristics are all brought out in each life and career segment.

Patterns are the most efficient and useful source of valid interpretation. You need only a few years of work experience and three conscientious passes through your notes to comprehend the most important patterns.

3. ASSUME THAT STRENGTHS CAN BECOME SHORTCOMINGS

Under pressure, we all tend to overuse our strengths, and, at times, they can result in predictable shortcomings. *During* the interview, you should remain alert to this possibility and ask enough questions to confirm or disconfirm if, for example, the:

♦ Highly cautious analyst misses too many valuable opportunities
♦ Glib salesperson talks around questions raised by bosses
♦ Warm, easy-going customer service representative becomes easily dominated
♦ Thorough planner is sometimes indecisive
♦ Person bent on self-development ignores the job

4. UNDERSTAND THAT RECENT PAST BEHAVIOR IS THE BEST PREDICTOR OF NEAR FUTURE BEHAVIOR

Behavior has inertia. Success patterns and failure patterns persist (though Axiom 6 will suggest ways of spotting potential behavioral changes).

If a person was a goof-off in college but for the past 10 years has been responsible, mature, and self-disciplined, the previous adolescent immaturity can generally be disregarded. If, on the other hand, a person was stable and responsible for 20 years and in the past year has undergone a midlife crisis that has resulted in three job changes and two wife changes, watch out! The desperate gambles, shallow self-insights, greed, dishonesty, and whatever else contributed to parts of such volatility in the recent past are apt to continue in the near future.

5. ASSUME ALL BEHAVIOR IS MOTIVATED

Psychologists get into a lot of trouble and leave themselves vulnerable to a lot of joking when they claim that every word, body movement, car accident, gesture, slip of the tongue, every constructive or destructive action with another human being, every success or failure, is motivated either consciously or unconsciously. Do unresolved childhood needs really manifest themselves in behaviors 45 years later, perhaps without the individual's even being aware of such controlling influences? (Did my toilet training make me a better controller or a messy impressionistic painter?)

As a first-year graduate student in psychology, I chuckled at what seemed such blatant absurdity and believed that such tenets were conveniently manufactured by insecure, socially maladjusted psychologists. In the intervening years, I have come to believe that everything an individual does or says does have some adaptive or need-fulfillment value, whether or not the person is conscious of it and whether or not it seems rational.

I have studied a great many videotaped selection interviews, and I've seen my businesspeople trainees become true believers in the all-behavior-is-motivated tenet. We analyze a tape and summarize our conclusions with substantiating data. We study the tape a second, a third, and sometimes a fourth time, and progressively deeper meanings to words, pauses, and nonverbal behaviors leap off the tape. We peel away surface knowledge like layers of an onion in gaining deeper and deeper insights. Every comment, pause, and facial expression "fits" what on video increasingly appears to be behavior that is 100 percent motivated.

The point, of course, is not to videotape interviews (that should be done only for training purposes) but to:

♦ *Take notes conscientiously,* not only with regard to what the person is saying, but *how* the person is saying it

♦ *Review the notes several times* before trying to formulate final conclusions

"Like, I'd like a job that self-actualizes, offers day care and affirms the environment."

6. SPOT RED FLAGS AND LOOK FOR EXPLANATIONS

There are a number of "red-flag" warning signals by which the interviewer can sense that some strong negative feeling is occurring within the interviewee and that further investigation is important for correct interpretation. Such signals include:

♦ Blushing

♦ Overly involved and complex responses, which usually sound well planned and rehearsed

♦ Sudden loss of what had been good eye contact

♦ Any significant change in pace (speeding up or slowing down)

♦ Suddenly higher or lower voice

♦ Inappropriate use of humor

♦ Any sudden change in voice volume (louder or softer)

♦ Sudden twitching, stammering, frowning, drumming fingers

♦ Suddenly more formal (rehearsed?) vocabulary

♦ Inconsistency between words and nonverbal behavior (if the candidate says, "I was happy there," and frowns while shaking his head as if to communicate "No, I wasn't," believe the nonverbal cues, not the words)

♦ Fumbling for a cigarette or something to drink (whereas previously there had not been fumbling)

♦ Sudden heavy perspiring

♦ Unusually long pauses (for the individual)

It is important to make note of any of these red flags. For long pauses, I simply record a dot every five seconds. At the time, I may not have the foggiest idea what is going on—is this person suddenly anxious, nervous, angry, or scared? Is the person trying to conceal some shortcoming or failure? Maybe, and maybe not.

When red flags occur, I go on a "fishing expedition," using follow-up questions to try to arrive at proper interpretation. Usually the individual is trying to conceal something, and that something is a shortcoming. Early in the interview, my fishing expedition is cursory; I don't want to risk destroying professional rapport. I ask a follow-up question or two and might make a note to myself to come back later to explore the issue more aggressively.

Late in the interview, professional rapport should be sufficiently strong to endure more direct questioning. Unresolved red flags will leave any interviewer with a queasy feeling, a hunch that there is a major unidentified weakness lurking in the interviewee. Probing deeper may harm rapport, but failure to do so will probably result in no job offer.

A comment about interpreting nonverbal behavior is appropriate here: *Don't overdo it!* There are a number of books on the subject, and they are generally worth reading, so long as you do not go overboard. Crossing one's arms does not necessarily mean a person is becoming defensive. It may mean that blood has accumulated in the extremities and crossing the arms lessens physical discomfort in the hands. (On the other hand, if the interviewee does not like your line of questioning and punches you in the nose, interpretation of nonverbal behavior is not very difficult.)

7. ASSUME THAT PEOPLE CAN CHANGE ... BEHAVIORS

Trying to figure out whether or not people will change is a topic on which everyone has an opinion. At presentations to boards of directors (usually about the talents and potentials of executives), inevitably a board member will ask, "Brad, do people change?"

It's a "glass half full or half empty" sort of question, and my response is: "People in their forties or older rarely change basic character, though a heart attack, death in the family, or business disaster can, as we have all observed, cause permanent change. People certainly change gradually—mature, mellow, and the like, and good mentors can accelerate growth curves. Eighty percent of executives I have counseled with have shown significant, positive changes in behavior—not character—one year later."

Do you "buy it" when an interviewee says, "I know there was a problem, but from now on, I'm going to be better organized," "more in control of my emotions," "a harder worker," "a better listener," "a nicer guy," or "a stronger manager"? It takes either guts or gullibility to believe that people will be happy and successful in job situations requiring dramatic and immediate improvement in a weak area, or a radical shift in values or needs.

If a person has been criticized by three employers (including the current one) in the past six years for missing deadlines, don't bet on the person's suddenly being able to improve priority setting or organization or whatever accounts for the previous problems. If a person has been a heavy-handed autocrat for years, don't readily accept the congenial interview personality and sincere sounding commitments to treating people better. An awareness of what to improve is certainly not sufficient for change. Although a new position offers a fresh start for someone to try to improve, usually the opposite occurs: People may initially be on good behavior in the new job, but when pressures mount, they regress to the old ways.

I believe that it is sometimes possible, in light of a specific person's shortcomings, to design a job that will minimize those shortcomings. Unless you make special efforts, however, don't count on anyone's turning over a new leaf. It is prudent to expect change only when you have *reason* to expect it.

> ***Assume people will change when they have already established a pattern of change.***

Signs of Change Potential

It sounds facetious to say that people can change when they have changed, but it's true. If an alcoholic has been off the bottle for two years, that's a compelling sign. Six months would probably not be so convincing. Ten years would be almost entirely convincing.

Growth begets growth—constructive change begets constructive change. Assume continued change when the interviewee:

♦ Has generally been successful in life
♦ Has good insights into his or her strengths and shortcomings
♦ Is bright
♦ Exhibits achievement motivation
♦ Shows very little or no defensiveness
♦ Has clearly demonstrated the capacity to correct small shortcomings before they become major weaknesses

In short, I'll bet on a person to turn over a new leaf when the individual has shown a history, particularly a recent history, of turning over new leaves.

"Can you be assertive?"

Nasty Joe and Meek Mike—Can They Change?

If you had to hire one of two people equal in all respects, except that one is so aggressive, hard-charging, and results-oriented that he is often blunt and tactless (Nasty Joe) and the other is unaggressive, passive, and shy (Meek Mike), and if success for either one would require overcoming the respective shortcoming (tactlessness for Nasty Joe and unassertiveness for Meek Mike) which one would you hire? I'd recommend Nasty Joe and here is why: Meek Mike has not developed the assertiveness "muscles" to exercise, even if he wanted to, but Nasty Joe already has the ability to be tactful, at least sometimes.

Nasty Joe knows how to be diplomatic. In a meeting yesterday with the chairman, Nasty Joe was quite gracious and compliant. At his daughter's wedding, he was a paragon of compassion. When he heard that a subordinate had terminal cancer, he was understanding, a good listener, and temporarily stopped using threats with that person. Nasty Joe merely has to use more of certain behaviors he already has in his repertoire and restrain a few of the more outrageous behaviors, before he can be perceived as a much improved manager. He may not actually change his personality, but it may seem that way to others.

Each year, I work with a dozen or so "Nasty Joes," and almost all have improved. I provide feedback on how behaviors are perceived in the work environment, and the Nasty Joes improve themselves. It's preferable if Nasty Joe sincerely wants to improve, but the techniques work even if he is just going through the motions in order to get his boss off his back. The technique I use is to survey Joe's co-workers (usually subordinates), getting ratings and comments on what they see as Joe's strengths and possible areas for improvement. Then I sit down with Joe to analyze the data and set goals for improvement. Nasty Joe is usually quite pleased with himself when surveys six months and one year later document his great improvement. He usually reports that the new behaviors are no longer playacted, but have become quite sincere. His subordinates stop covering up mistakes and begin to tell him when problems are arising. Finally, turnover is usually down and morale up. These are the sorts of things that register with Nasty Joe, so that some of the changes actually become permanent.

A Meek Mike may want to change, but he is not immediately able to, even if his job is on the line. When Meek Mike tries to become dramatically more assertive, it is usually so awkward, ludicrous, or offensive that the effort is ineffective.

It is probably smart not to hire anyone if a 5 percent or greater behavioral change is required to overcome meekness, or if a 15 percent or greater change in throttling aggressiveness is required. These percentages are not based on scientific research—just my impression that it's easier to file down Nasty Joe's rough edges than it is to build aggressiveness in a Meek Mike.

8. LOOK FOR ATTRIBUTIONS AND EVALUATION

Knowing that a person worked 13 hours a day, 7 days a week for a year can be important, but knowing how the person *felt* about workload can be even more important. Learning if the person felt burned out after a week or "couldn't get enough of this interesting challenge" even after one year, could be essential for accurate interpretation.

The Guide directs you to ask what the interviewee believes were high points and low points, successes and failures, accomplishments and disappointments, why each employment situation was liked or disliked, what is desired in a new job, and how co-workers would judge various actions. These questions produce rich, meaningful data because they require the interviewee to evaluate—to express feelings and needs.

Although the Guide guarantees that the interviewer will have evaluative judgments available for interpretation, it obviously does not contain follow-up questions and useful tangents to pursue. My advice for when you meander away from the Guide is not just to find out what occurred in the interviewee's life, but constantly to ask what the interviewee thought of this, what was liked, and what was disliked.

To what does the individual attribute success or failure? What motives does the interviewee attribute to subordinates, peers, superiors, and others? Determining attributions provides a rich source of interpretive data. If, in reviewing his own 20-year career, it seems to the interviewee that his career progress has been consistently hampered because of other people's stupidity, insensitivity, greed, or selfishness, it is likely that some or all of the problem is with the interviewee.

9. WEIGH NEGATIVES MORE HEAVILY THAN POSITIVES

The advice to emphasize the negative may seem like heresy in a culture committed to positive mental attitude. In most organizations, at higher levels (not entry level or individual performance jobs), a *lack of negatives* is one of the most important factors in success.

> ***People succeed not so much because of full utilization of strengths, but because of their lack of significant shortcomings.***

A "negative" is simply a factor in which the individual does not fit the job. It does not make the person "bad."

> ***"Good fit" factors do not assure success, but "no-fit" factors can assure failure.***

Bookstores are loaded with books giving career advice, and very often the advice is to think positively, determine your strengths, work hard to maximize those strengths, and don't pay much attention to shortcomings. That is not bad advice for someone on an assembly line or even a technical professional position up to, but not including, first-level supervision. If a chemist, for example, is bright, responsible, dedicated, and knowledgeable, just about all that is necessary for success is to build on those strengths.

Once a person progresses to management, however, the game changes. Others are doing more of the technical work, and a greater percentage of time is spent planning, organizing, staffing, directing, and controlling.

A person strongly motivated to rise to upper management positions can be compared with someone in a rowboat race. For an electrical engineer fresh out of college, there is only a little leaky hole for technical expertise, but if the person does not conscientiously work to fill in the hole, it will get bigger because the expertise of electrical engineers is outdated very quickly. Once the individual gets to a mid-management position, technical expertise might not be so important, and the wood around the hole will swell enough to fill the hole completely. However, technical prowess is ordinarily a major factor contributing to promotion through management, so it can't be ignored at the beginning of the race. There can be other holes—knowledge of time management, salesmanship, how to recruit, how to train people. There are numerous holes having to do with general business knowledge—marketing, finance, operations, personnel, business law. It's not so much the hard rowers who finally win the race to the executive suite; it's the reasonably hard rowers who do a reasonably good job of plugging most of the holes who finally get there.

As I look back over the records of thousands of executives I have evaluated, there is one inescapable conclusion: The only truly distinguishing characteristic of consistently successful executives in large, publicly owned companies is *lack of major liabilities*. Executives are usually bright (though rarely geniuses), their work habits are good (although commonly a little disorganized), and they are usually effective managers (although some are a little too tough and others a little too soft, and most don't offer sufficient praise and recognition). The successful executives are usually politically aware (though not necessarily master gamesplayers) and have a good appearance (although usually not supercharismatic). Eight times out of 10, however, they are not very dumb, not technically incompetent, not very disorganized, not politically naive, and really *not very anything that is negative*.

The same point can be made in terms of person specifications. The Guide and appendices in this book use a rating scale in which 4 = excellent, 3 = Good, 2 = Only Fair, 1 = Poor, and 0 = Very Poor. Across a broad range of person specifications, people in management get and deserve promotion with:

> A few 4s
> Mostly 3s
> Very Few 2s
> No 1s
> No 0s

Occasionally, a high-talent, high-risk person is selected over a "sure" good performer, but not very often. Hiring or promoting someone with a gross deficiency that is not easily compensated for is like betting on a decathlon athlete who cannot pole vault: that person can perhaps beat weak competition, but rarely can succeed in world-class competition.

For these reasons, it is important for interviewers to focus interpretive sights not only on the positives, but particularly keenly on the negatives. Shortcomings and liabilities, even minor ones, will probably contribute disproportionately to any failures that might occur in the position you are filling.

10. WATCH FOR STRONG FEELINGS AND BELIEFS

What is your hunch about an interviewee who repeatedly makes adamant statements impugning the integrity of people? After a while, you start wondering about the candidate's honesty, right?

People sometimes have strongest feelings about issues they deeply fear —in themselves. A study decades ago found that Marines who regularly beat up homosexuals were—guess what—latent homosexuals. Sometimes preachers preach loudest about their own sins.

> ***Methinks she doth protest too much ...***
>
> William Shakespeare

Of course, having strong beliefs can be a candidate's strongest asset. It's when beliefs are accompanied by rigidity and intolerance that you should begin to wonder if there are accompanying shortcomings.

♦ "Insensitive people drive me absolutely *crazy.*"
♦ "If there's one thing I *can't stand,* it's intolerance."
♦ "I'm *unalterably* opposed to men and women traveling together."
♦ "I could *never* work for an autocrat."

The pattern that suggests a flaw in the interviewee is one in which the interviewee repeatedly rails against that particular flaw in others.

A selection interview is rarely an emotionally charged event with dramatic expressions of feeling. When unusually strong emotion enters, ask yourself: Why is this belief not calmly stated—why does this issue grate so deeply?

As the interview unfolds, the pattern of beliefs emerges clearer and clearer. A person's beliefs govern behavior. The pattern of successes and failures, job changes, risks taken, paints an increasingly clear portrait of a person.

> ***If you don't change your beliefs, your life will be like this forever. Is that good news?***

The boxed maxim is a key to interpretation. During and after the interview, it is useful for the interviewer to:

♦ Step back (mentally)
♦ Ask what this interviewee is disclosing about beliefs
♦ Assume that strongly held beliefs are not very amenable to change
♦ Test hunches that what the interviewee dislikes most in others may be disliked or feared in him- or herself

11. DON'T BELIEVE IN COINCIDENCES IN RESPONSES

The warning against "coincidences" is an offshoot of "all behavior is motivated," and can be explained in a true story:

A recently hired VP Distribution for one of the largest companies in the world mentioned the Mafia repeatedly in an interview. The Guide has no specific questions about the Mob, so the fact that, in describing his career history, specific situations happened to involve the Mafia caught my attention.

Toward the end of the interview, I asked directly, "Have you had recent involvement with Mafioso?" After a long pause, I got a response I'll never forget. In order to get out of nasty labor contracts, the head of the union (then in jail) suggested an "arrangement" with a labor consulting firm that would, for a price, guarantee more favorable contracts. My interviewee had met with union representatives, who happened to have been reputed hit-men (hit-persons?).

"Was the President aware of your discussions with these thugs?"

"No."

"O.K. Let's go talk with him, now."

The President asked if the Chairman was aware. "No." So the three of us marched into the Chairman's office. He killed the proposal instantly.

"Do you have any special skills?"

There are no "coincidences" in interviews. Achievement-oriented "doers" talk freely about achievements. Burned-out workaholics will bring into the interview frequent references to stress. People who like golf a lot more than work will say so, indirectly—by continuing to bring up what a great day for golf it is, what an exciting U.S. Open occurred last month, and how hard it is to keep one's mind on work when new golf clubs have just been delivered. Use of "The In-Depth Selection Interview Guide" permits important character clues to come out unwittingly—but clearly—in "asides."

12. DON'T LEAP TO CONCLUSIONS

Interviewers leap to erroneous conclusions. In my earlier book,[1] I summarize research on the halo effect, overweighting first impression, biases, stereotypes, projection, and failure to quantify, and the clear message is that most interviewers leap to erroneous conclusions, at enormous cost to them, their employer, and those mishired. Having trained thousands of interviewers, my hunch is that high achievers are so accustomed to making quick judg-

---

[1] Brad Smart, *Selection Interviewing: A Management Psychologist's Recommended Approach,* John Wiley & Son, 1983.

ments and so ignorant of how to interview that they fall victim to those major sources of interviewer error.

The quickness of interviewers to reject a candidate is also a by-product of the achiever's tendency to be critical of self and others. I've asked more than 10,000 managers, "Did you do your best last year?" and less than 1 percent replied affirmatively. I've asked, "Did you *try* your best?" and the majority said, "No." (Stay with me on this, because if you are a high achiever, I'm talking about *you*.) If you are so chronically self-critical as to feel you neither did nor even tried your best, my guess is that you project your sense of failure onto interviewees, and fail to evaluate them accurately.

Interviewers are constantly overestimating or underestimating interviewees because of the tendencies to judge quickly and to project their own insecurities.

I'm not suggesting that you abandon your achievement orientation. Unfacetiously, I regularly say insecure overachievers make the business world go around because no matter how high is the bar, they always want to raise it. However, in selection interviewing, it is smart to:

♦ Conduct a full in-depth interview of finalists, using the Guide
♦ Conscientiously take notes of successes and failures
♦ Withhold judgment until sufficient interview data are available

To withhold judgment, you are advised to hypothesize, at least for the purpose of interviewing, that *everyone tries his best all the time*. Operate on this belief, and your normal, understandable inclination to selectively perceive and selectively weight interview responses will be better contained. The advantages of maintaining this new perspective are:

1. It's easier to be objective as an interviewer. If you catch yourself thinking, "This guy's a jerk" and substitute, "Wait a minute, he is (and was) trying his best to run his life," you can keep your own hangups from closing your mind.

2. You will be proud of yourself. Interviewers who discipline themselves to evaluate but not "judge" people know they are being fair in interviews.
   Of course, as an interviewer you may calibrate the interviewee's technical skills (or whatever) to be sub-par, and consequently choose not to extend a job offer. As soon as you add, "You jerk, how could you have failed to keep up technically," you have determined that you are superior to this turkey, and unconsciously give yourself

permission to selectively perceive more negatives in the person than actually exist.

3. You will be a more accurate predictor of job success. As such, you will improve your hiring "batting average," and minimize those costly mishires.

4. You will be more successful in developing the people you hire. With the wealth of insight into a new hire's strengths, weaker points, and potentials, *now* is the best time to carve out a developmental plan.

> ***The best interviewers interpret critically, without "judging" a fellow human being.***

FINAL COMMENT

The dozen aphorisms in this chapter concerning the "how to's" of interpreting interviewee responses do not run counter to what you have observed and learned in your management career. You know that people have patterns of behavior, and that in many cases these patterns are very resistant to change.

Interviewees often say much more than they realize they are saying, to the ears of a trained interviewer. When you interpret what is said through the assumptions set forth here, you will have an excellent chance of avoiding a mishire. And because the Guide questions that prompt the revelations are on legally solid ground, you will have little fear of reprisal for not hiring. But that topic is for the next chapter....

Legal Considerations

Interviewers are legitimately concerned with legal constraints. Ask the wrong question and your corporation lawyers promise you embarrassment and, perhaps, three to five years in a minimum security prison.

However, if you are among the majority of managers who basically wants to do the right thing, and you make a little effort to learn and comply with the various equal opportunity laws, life may not be nearly as complex or frustrating as it is for a manager who chooses to ignore the law.

The topic of legal considerations in hiring is too complex for adequate coverage in a brief handbook. This chapter, though, does present a chart of dos and don'ts prepared by the U.S. Equal Employment Opportunity Commission (August, 1981).

Ask your Human Resources representative to get you a summary of interviewing implications of the following pertinent laws:

- Title VII of Civil Rights Act of 1964

- The Immigration Reform and Control Act of 1986

- Age Discrimination in Employment Act

- Vocational Rehabilitation Act

- Vietnam Era Veterans' Readjustment Assistance Act

- The Privacy Act (1974)

- The Fair Credit and Reporting Act (1970)

- The Family Education Rights and Privacy Act, and Buckley Amendment (1974)

- Freedom of Information Act (1966)

GENERAL GUIDELINES

If the questions you ask stem logically from the applicant's background relative to the prerequisites of the job in question, there is little danger in getting into trouble for asking them. The application form reproduced in Appendix C does not seek any information that is currently considered illegal. The "In-Depth Selection Interview Guide" questions are equally circumspect. It is important that you *choose questions* from the Guide (and frame any additional questions of your own) *on the basis of person specifications based on a carefully developed job description*. For example, emphasis on college experience is misplaced if the job cannot be shown to require higher education.

Even if a question *is* job-relevant, it should not be asked only of specific (protected) classes of people, such as females or Hispanics.

The legal considerations of reference checking were covered in Chapter 6. In general, confidentiality and securing permission are vital. Questions that would be inappropriate for a candidate interview should not be asked of a reference.

The following section gives specific guidelines established by the Equal Employment Opportunity Commission as to what subjects can be covered—or not covered—under what circumstances.

EEOC GUIDELINES

SUBJECT	ILLEGAL	LEGAL
Race, Color, Religion, National Origin	All unexplained direct or indirect inquiries may be evidence of bias. State laws may expressly prohibit.	Employers may lawfully collect such information for affirmative action programs, government recordkeeping, and reporting requirements, or studies to promote EEO recruiting and testing. Employers must be able to prove these legitimate business purposes and keep this information separate from regular employee records.
Height and Weight	If minorities or women more often disqualified and meeting height or weight limits not necessary for safe job performance.	

SUBJECT	ILLEGAL	LEGAL
Marital Status, Children, Child Care	Non-job related and illegal if used to discriminate against women. Illegal to ask only (or have different policies for) women.	If information is needed for tax, insurance, or Social Security purposes, get it *after* employment.
English Language Skill	If not necessary for job and minorities more often disqualified.	
Education Requirements	If not directly job-related or no business necessity is proven and minorities more often disqualified.	
Friends or Relatives Working for Employer	Preference for friends or relatives of current workers, if this reduces opportunities for women or minorities. Nepotism policies barring hire of friends or relatives of current workers, if this reduces opportunities for women or men or for minorities.	
Arrest Records	If no subsequent convictions and no proof of business necessity. Mere request for, without consideration of, arrest record is illegal.	
Conviction Records		Only if their number, nature, and recentness are considered in determining applicant's suitability. Inquiries should state that record isn't absolute bar and such factors as age and time of offense, seriousness and nature of violation, and rehabilitation will be taken into account.
Military Service Discharge	Honorable discharge requirement, if minorities more often disqualified.	If information is used to determine if further background check is necessary.

115

SUBJECT	ILLEGAL	LEGAL
Military Service Discharge	EEOC says employers should not, as matter of policy, reject applicants with less than honorable discharges, and inquiry re military record should be avoided unless business necessity is shown.	Inquiries should state that less than honorable discharge isn't absolute bar to employment and other factors will affect final hiring decision.
Citizenship	If has purpose or effect of discriminating on basis of national origin. Note: Questions relating to citizenship must also comply with requirements of the Immigration Reform and Control Act of 1986.	Legal aliens, eligible to work, may be discriminated against in interest of national security or under federal law or presidential order concerning the particular position or premises.
Economic Status	Inquiries re poor credit rating are unlawful, if no business necessity is shown. Other inquiries re financial status—bankruptcy, car, or home ownership, garnishments—may likewise be illegal because of disparate impact on minorities.	
Availability for Holiday/ Weekend Work		If employer can show that questions have no exclusionary effect on employees/applicants who need accommodations for their religious practices, that questions are otherwise justified, and that no alternatives with less exclusionary effect are available.
Data Required for Legitimate Business Purposes		Information on marital status, number and age of children, etc., necessary for insurance, reporting requirements, and other business purposes should be obtained *after* the person is employed. "Tear-off sheets," preferably anonymous, which are separated from application forms before the applications are processed, are also lawful.

APPENDIX
A

*The In-Depth
Selection
Interview Guide*

In-Depth Selection
INTERVIEW GUIDE

Bradford D. Smart, Ph.D.

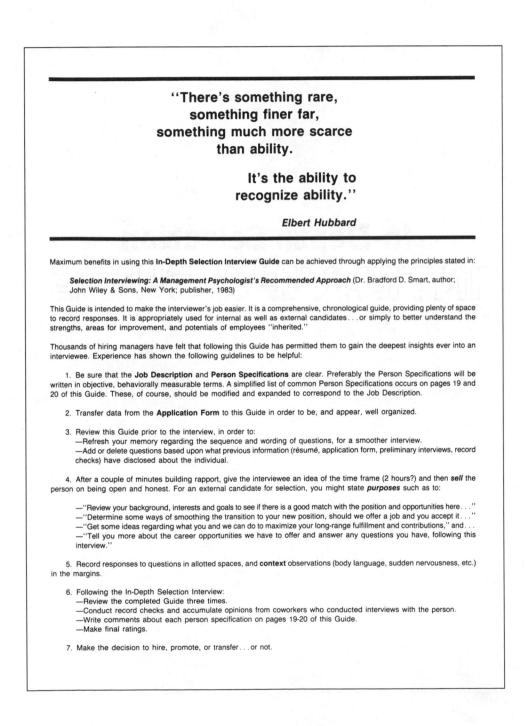

> **"There's something rare,
> something finer far,
> something much more scarce
> than ability.**
>
> **It's the ability to
> recognize ability."**
>
> *Elbert Hubbard*

Maximum benefits in using this **In-Depth Selection Interview Guide** can be achieved through applying the principles stated in:

> *Selection Interviewing: A Management Psychologist's Recommended Approach* (Dr. Bradford D. Smart, author; John Wiley & Sons, New York; publisher, 1983)

This Guide is intended to make the interviewer's job easier. It is a comprehensive, chronological guide, providing plenty of space to record responses. It is appropriately used for internal as well as external candidates . . . or simply to better understand the strengths, areas for improvement, and potentials of employees "inherited."

Thousands of hiring managers have felt that following this Guide has permitted them to gain the deepest insights ever into an interviewee. Experience has shown the following guidelines to be helpful:

1. Be sure that the **Job Description** and **Person Specifications** are clear. Preferably the Person Specifications will be written in objective, behaviorally measurable terms. A simplified list of common Person Specifications occurs on pages 19 and 20 of this Guide. These, of course, should be modified and expanded to correspond to the Job Description.

2. Transfer data from the **Application Form** to this Guide in order to be, and appear, well organized.

3. Review this Guide prior to the interview, in order to:
   —Refresh your memory regarding the sequence and wording of questions, for a smoother interview.
   —Add or delete questions based upon what previous information (résumé, application form, preliminary interviews, record checks) have disclosed about the individual.

4. After a couple of minutes building rapport, give the interviewee an idea of the time frame (2 hours?) and then **sell** the person on being open and honest. For an external candidate for selection, you might state **purposes** such as to:

   —"Review your background, interests and goals to see if there is a good match with the position and opportunities here . . ."
   —"Determine some ways of smoothing the transition to your new position, should we offer a job and you accept it . . ."
   —"Get some ideas regarding what you and we can do to maximize your long-range fulfillment and contributions," and . . .
   —"Tell you more about the career opportunities we have to offer and answer any questions you have, following this interview."

5. Record responses to questions in allotted spaces, and **context** observations (body language, sudden nervousness, etc.) in the margins.

6. Following the In-Depth Selection Interview:
   —Review the completed Guide three times.
   —Conduct record checks and accumulate opinions from coworkers who conducted interviews with the person.
   —Write comments about each person specification on pages 19-20 of this Guide.
   —Make final ratings.

7. Make the decision to hire, promote, or transfer . . . or not.

EDUCATION

So that I can get a good feel for your background—your education, work experience, and the like—let's *briefly* go back to your high school days and come forward chronologically, up to the present. Then we'll talk about your plans and goals for the future.

HIGH SCHOOL

Note to Interviewer: If you are uncomfortable beginning with high school years, skip this section.

1. I see from the Application Form that you attended _____ (high school), graduating in _____ (year). Would you please expand on the Application Form information and give me a **brief rundown** on your high school years. . . particularly events that might have affected later career decisions. I'd be interested in knowing about **work experiences,** what the school was like, what you were like back then, the curriculum, activities, how you did in school, high and low points, and so forth. (Ask the following questions to obtain complete information not included in responses to the general "smorgasbord" question.)

2. Give me a feel for what **kind of school** it was (if necessary, specify large/small, rural/urban, cliquish, etc.), and generally, what your high school years were like.

_____
_____
_____
_____
_____

3. What was your **curriculum?** (general, technical, or college preparatory)?

_____

4. What school **activities** did you take part in? (Note activities listed on Application Form.)

_____
_____
_____
_____

5. What sort of **grades** did you receive, what was your class standing and what were your study habits like? (Confirm data on Application Form.)

GPA: _____ / _____ (scale)   Class Standing: _____ out of _____

Study Habits _____   SAT Scores _____   ACT Scores _____

6. What **people** or events might have had an influence on your career?

_____
_____
_____ _____
_____

7. Were there any class **offices, awards, honors,** or special achievements during your high school days? (Note Application Form responses.)

_____
_____
_____
_____

8. What were **high points** during your high school days?

_____
_____
_____
_____
_____

9. What were **low points**, or **least enjoyable occurences,** during your high school days? (Were you ever suspended, did you ever crack up a car, did you have any serious illnesses?)

_____
_____
_____
_____

10. Give me a feel for any **jobs** you held during high school—the types of jobs, whether they were during the school year or summer, hours worked, and any high or low points associated with them. (If the person did not work during the summer, ask how the summer months were spent.)

_____
_____
_____
_____

13. (TRANSITION QUESTION) What were your **career thoughts** toward the end of high school?

Note: Transition Questions have to do with important choices in life—what to do, when, how to go about it. The answers are often very revealing, not only about the individual at the time those choices were made, but about the person's current attitudes regarding those transition decisions and current values. So, probe very thoroughly whenever major life directions were established or altered.

_____
_____
_____
_____

COLLEGE (UNDERGRADUATE)

1. Now about your **undergraduate** days. I notice that you attended _____ (name of college) from _____ until _____ earning a _____ degree. **Why** was that particular school selected? (If more than one school was attended, ask this and subsequent questions about each one.)

_____
_____
_____
_____

2. Would you give me the same sort of **highlights** about those years as you did for high school . . . what you did, how you did, and how you liked it. (Confirm Application Form data. Ask the following questions to obtain complete information not included in answers to the general ''smorgasbord'' question.)

_____
_____
_____

3. Generally, what were your college years like?

_____
_____

4. What sort of **curriculum** did you focus on? (Follow-up: Exactly what major(s), and why were there any changes in majors?)

_____
_____

5. What sort of campus **activities** did you get involved in? (Follow-up: What was your level of involvement—member, leader, or what?)

_____
_____
_____
_____

6. I see that you earned a _____ (GPA). How would you describe your **study habits** during college? (Look for clues as to amount of effort expended.)

_____
_____
_____

7. Please give me a feel for any **work experiences** you had during college—the types of jobs, whether they were during the school years or summers, hours per week worked, and any high or low points. (If not in campus activities, and there were no work experiences, determine how spare time during the school year and how summer months were spent.)

_____
_____
_____

8. What were important **career influences**?

_____
_____

9. What were **high points** during your undergraduate days?

_____
_____
_____
_____

10. What were **low points,** or **least enjoyable occurrences,** during your undergraduate days?

_____
_____
_____
_____

11. (TRANSITION QUESTION) I see from your Application Form that following college you (attended graduate school, got a job at X company, or whatever). What were your **career thoughts** toward the end of college? What were the options considered?

_____
_____
_____
_____
_____
_____

GRADUATE SCHOOL

1. _____ 2. _____ 3. _____
             School   Date Attended   Degree

4. Why this school and degree _____
_____

5. High Points _____
_____

6. Low Points _____
_____

7. Career Thoughts _____
_____

WORK HISTORY

Now I would like you to tell me about your work history. There are a lot of things I would like to know about each position. Let me tell you what these things are now, so I won't have to interrupt you so often. We already have some of this information from your Application Form and previous discussions. Of course I need to know the **employer, location, dates** of employment, your **titles,** and **salary** history. I would also be interested in knowing what your **expectations** were for each job, whether they were met, what major **challenges** you faced, how they were handled, and what were the **most** and **least enjoyable** aspects of each job. I also want to know what you feel were your greatest **accomplishments** and significant **mistakes** or disappointments, what each **supervisor** was like and what you would **guess** each supervisor really felt were your strengths and weaker points. Finally, I would like to know the circumstances under which you **left** each position.

Note: If the person worked for a single employer and had, say, three jobs with that employer, consider each one of those a *separate* position, and complete a Work History Form on it. Following is suggested wording for information requested on the Work History Form:

1. What was the name of the **employer, location,** and **dates** of employment? (Get a ''feel'' for the organization by asking about volume sales, number of employees, products or services, and profitability.)

2. What was your job **title**?

3. What were the starting and final levels of **compensation**?

4. What were your **expectations** for the job?

5. What were your **responsibilities** and accountabilities?

6. What results were achieved in terms of **successes** and **accomplishments**? (As time permits, get specifics, such as individual or shared accomplishment, barriers overcome, ''bottom line'' results, and impact on career—bonus, promotability, performance review.)

7. We all make **mistakes**—what would you say were mistakes or failures experienced in this job? (As time permits, get specifics.)

8. All jobs seem to have their pluses and minuses; what were the **most enjoyable** or rewarding aspects of this job?

9. What were the **least enjoyable** aspects of the job?

10. To what extent did **luck**—that is, fortunate or unfortunate circumstances beyond your control—enter into your record of performance?

11. What **circumstances** contributed to your leaving? (Always probe for *other* reasons.)

12. What was your **supervisor's name** and title? Where is that person now? May I contact him/her?

13. What is/was it like working for (him/her) and what were (his/her) **strengths** and **shortcomings** as a supervisor, from your point of view?

14. What is your **best guess** as to what (supervisor's name) honestly felt were/are your **strengths, weaker points,** and **overall performance**?

Note: When it it is learned what the ''next job'' was, a useful question is, ''Would you please tell me *what you did, how you did,* and *how you liked it?*''

WORK HISTORY FORM 1

1. _____
   Employer   Starting dates (mo./yr.)   Final (mo./yr.)

   _____
   Location   Type of business
   Description _____
2. Title _____
3. Salary (Starting) _____ Final _____
4. Expectations _____
   _____
   _____
5. Responsibilities/Accountabilities _____
   _____
   _____
6. Successes/Accomplishments _____
   _____
   _____
   _____
   _____
   _____
7. Failures/Mistakes _____
   _____
8. Most Enjoyable _____
   _____
9. Least Enjoyable _____
   _____
10. Luck _____
11. Reasons for Leaving _____
    _____
    _____

SUPERVISOR

12. _____
    Supervisor's name   Title

    _____
    Where now   Permission to contact?
13. Appraisal of Supervisor
    His/Her Strengths _____
    _____
    His/Her Shortcomings _____
    _____
14. Best guess as to what he/she really felt at that time were your

Strengths	Weaker Points

    Overall Performance _____
    _____

WORK HISTORY FORM 2

1. _____
   Employer   Starting dates (mo./yr.)   Final (mo./yr.)

   _____
   Location   Type of business
   Description _____

2. Title _____

3. Salary (Starting) _____ Final_____

4. Expectations _____
   _____
   _____

5. Responsibilities/Accountabilities _____
   _____

6. Successes/Accomplishments _____
   _____
   _____
   _____
   _____
   _____

7. Failures/Mistakes _____
   _____

8. Most Enjoyable _____
   _____

9. Least Enjoyable _____
   _____

10. Luck _____

11. Reasons for Leaving _____
    _____
    _____

SUPERVISOR

12. _____
    Supervisor's name   Title

    _____
    Where now   Permission to contact?

13. Appraisal of Supervisor
    His/Her Strengths _____
    _____
    His/Her Shortcomings _____
    _____

14. Best guess as to what he/she really felt at that time were your

Strengths	Weaker Points

    Overall Performance _____
    _____

WORK HISTORY FORM 3

1. _____
   Employer   Starting dates (mo./yr.)   Final (mo./yr.)

   Location   Type of business
   Description _____
2. Title _____
3. Salary (Starting) _____ Final_____
4. Expectations _____
   _____
   _____
5. Responsibilities/Accountabilities _____
   _____
   _____
6. Successes/Accomplishments _____
   _____
   _____
   _____
   _____
   _____
7. Failures/Mistakes _____
   _____
8. Most Enjoyable _____
   _____
9. Least Enjoyable _____
   _____
10. Luck _____
11. Reasons for Leaving _____
    _____

SUPERVISOR

12. _____
    Supervisor's name   Title

    Where now   Permission to contact?
13. Appraisal of Supervisor
    His/Her Strengths _____
    _____
    His/Her Shortcomings _____
    _____
14. Best guess as to what he/she really felt at that time were your

Strengths	Weaker Points

    Overall Performance _____
    _____

WORK HISTORY FORM 4

1. _____
   Employer   Starting dates (mo./yr.)   Final (mo./yr.)

   _____
   Location   Type of business
   Description _____
2. Title _____
3. Salary (Starting) _____ Final_____
4. Expectations _____
   _____
   _____

5. Responsibilities/Accountabilities _____
   _____
   _____

6. Successes/Accomplishments _____
   _____
   _____
   _____
   _____
   _____

7. Failures/Mistakes _____
   _____
8. Most Enjoyable _____
   _____
9. Least Enjoyable _____
   _____

10. Luck _____
11. Reasons for Leaving _____
    _____
    _____

SUPERVISOR

12. _____
    Supervisor's name   Title

    _____
    Where now   Permission to contact?
13. Appraisal of Supervisor
    His/Her Strengths _____
    _____
    His/Her Shortcomings _____
    _____

14. Best guess as to what he/she really felt at that time were your

Strengths	Weaker Points

    Overall Performance _____
    _____

WORK HISTORY FORM 5

1. _____
   Employer   Starting dates (mo./yr.)   Final (mo./yr.)

   _____
   Location   Type of business

   Description _____

2. Title _____

3. Salary (Starting) _____ Final _____

4. Expectations _____
   _____
   _____

5. Responsibilities/Accountabilities _____
   _____
   _____

6. Successes/Accomplishments _____
   _____
   _____
   _____
   _____
   _____

7. Failures/Mistakes _____
   _____

8. Most Enjoyable _____
   _____

9. Least Enjoyable _____
   _____

10. Luck _____

11. Reasons for Leaving _____
    _____
    _____

SUPERVISOR

12. _____
    Supervisor's name   Title

    _____
    Where now   Permission to contact?

13. Appraisal of Supervisor
    His/Her Strengths _____
    _____

    His/Her Shortcomings _____
    _____

14. Best guess as to what he/she really felt at that time were your

Strengths	Weaker Points

Overall Performance _____
_____

WORK HISTORY FORM 6

1. _____
   Employer   Starting dates (mo./yr.)   Final (mo./yr.)

   _____
   Location   Type of business
   Description _____

2. Title _____

3. Salary (Starting) _____ Final _____

4. Expectations _____
   _____
   _____

5. Responsibilities/Accountabilities _____
   _____
   _____

6. Successes/Accomplishments _____
   _____
   _____
   _____
   _____
   _____
   _____

7. Failures/Mistakes _____
   _____

8. Most Enjoyable _____
   _____

9. Least Enjoyable _____
   _____

10. Luck _____

11. Reasons for Leaving _____
    _____
    _____

SUPERVISOR

12. _____
    Supervisor's name   Title

    _____
    Where now   Permission to contact?

13. Appraisal of Supervisor
    His/Her Strengths _____
    _____

    His/Her Shortcomings _____
    _____

14. Best guess as to what he/she really felt at that time were your

    _____ Strengths _____ | _____ Weaker Points _____

    Overall Performance _____
    _____

PLANS AND GOALS FOR THE FUTURE

1. Let's discuss what you are looking for in your **next job.** (Note "plans for the future" section of Application Form.)

_____
_____
_____
_____
_____
_____
_____

2. What are **other job possibilities,** and how do you feel about each one?

_____
_____
_____
_____
_____

3. What about **five** or **ten years** down the road; where do you hope to be by then, career-wise? (Possible follow up: Any wild ideas for jobs that might be fun to consider?)

_____
_____
_____
_____
_____

4. What do you view as **advantages** or possible **disadvantages** of joining us?

Advantages _____
_____
_____
_____
_____

Disadvantages _____
_____
_____
_____
_____

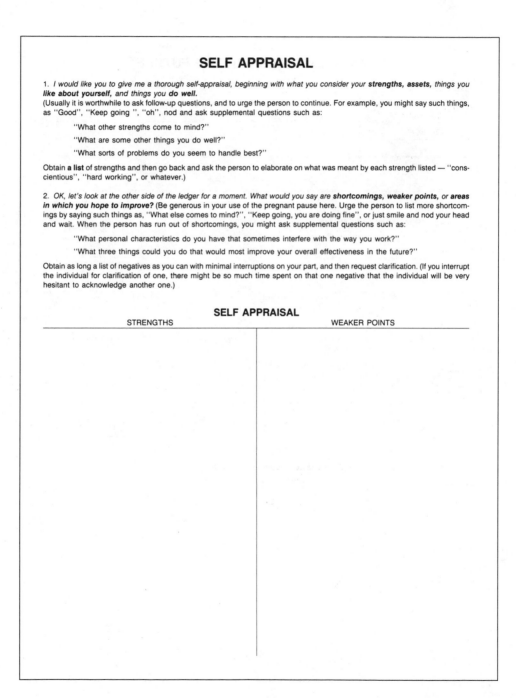

SELF APPRAISAL

1. *I would like you to give me a thorough self-appraisal, beginning with what you consider your* **strengths, assets,** *things you* **like about yourself,** *and things you* **do well.**
(Usually it is worthwhile to ask follow-up questions, and to urge the person to continue. For example, you might say such things, as "Good", "Keep going ", "oh", nod and ask supplemental questions such as:

"What other strengths come to mind?"

"What are some other things you do well?"

"What sorts of problems do you seem to handle best?"

Obtain **a list** of strengths and then go back and ask the person to elaborate on what was meant by each strength listed — "conscientious", "hard working", or whatever.)

2. *OK, let's look at the other side of the ledger for a moment. What would you say are* **shortcomings, weaker points,** *or* **areas in which you hope to improve?** (Be generous in your use of the pregnant pause here. Urge the person to list more shortcomings by saying such things as, "What else comes to mind?", "Keep going, you are doing fine", or just smile and nod your head and wait. When the person has run out of shortcomings, you might ask supplemental questions such as:

"What personal characteristics do you have that sometimes interfere with the way you work?"

"What three things could you do that would most improve your overall effectiveness in the future?"

Obtain as long a list of negatives as you can with minimal interruptions on your part, and then request clarification. (If you interrupt the individual for clarification of one, there might be so much time spent on that one negative that the individual will be very hesitant to acknowledge another one.)

SELF APPRAISAL

STRENGTHS	WEAKER POINTS

MANAGEMENT

1. How would you describe your **management philosophy** and **style**?

_____
_____
_____

2. What would you suppose your **subordinates** feel are your strengths and shortcomings, from their points of view?

STRENGTHS	SHORTCOMINGS

3. In what ways might you want to **modify** your approach to dealing with subordinates?

_____
_____

4. Would you please give me a **paragraph about each subordinate,** indicating title, length of employment, strengths, short-comings, and overall performance? (Note: Ask this question for *a couple of* positions. Before you leave this section, be sure you have a good feel for how many people were recruited and selected, what approaches were used, how the people were trained and developed, how each worked out in the job, and for those who did not work out well, what happened with them.)

_____
_____
_____
_____
_____
_____
_____
_____
_____
_____
_____
_____
_____
_____
_____
_____
_____
_____
_____
_____
_____
_____
_____
_____
_____
_____
_____
_____

FOCUSED QUESTIONS

The following questions for some person specifications are optional. Those with an asterisk (*) are routinely asked. Get specific examples, not general responses.

INTELLECTUAL CHARACTERISTICS

1. LEARNING ABILITY
   a. How would you describe your **learning ability**? In what kinds of situations are you fast or slow to learn? _____
   _____

2. ANALYSIS SKILLS
   *a. How would you describe your **problem analysis** skills?_____
   _____

   b. Do people generally regard you as one who diligently pursues every **detail** or do you tend to be more **broad brush**?
   _____
   _____

   c. What **analytic approaches** and tools do you use? _____
   _____

3. JUDGMENT
   *a. How would you describe your **decision-making** approach? Are you decisive and quick, but sometimes too quick, or are you more thorough, but sometimes too slow? Are you intuitive or do you go purely with the facts? Do you involve many or a few people? _____
   _____
   _____

   *b. What are a couple of the **most difficult or challenging** decisions you have made recently? _____
   _____

   *c. What are a couple of the **best** and **worst** decisions you have made in the past year? _____
   _____

   d. What **maxims** do you live by? _____
   _____

4. CONCEPTUAL SKILL
   a. Are you more comfortable dealing with **concrete**, tangible, short term, or more **abstract**, conceptual long term issues? (Please give specifics.) _____
   _____

5. CREATIVITY/INNOVATIVENESS
   *a. How **creative** are you? What are the best examples of your creativity? _____
   _____

6. STRATEGIC PLANNING
   a. Please describe your **experience** in strategic planning. _____
   _____

   b. Where do you **predict** that your (industry/function) is going in the next three years? What is the "conventional wisdom," and what are your own thoughts? _____
   _____

7. PRAGMATISM
   a. Do you consider yourself a more **visionary** or more **pragmagic** thinker. . .and why? _____
   _____

8. ORAL COMMUNICATION

   a. How would you rate yourself in **public speaking**? If we had a video tape of your most recent presentation, what would we see? _____

   *b. How would you describe your role in **meetings**—ones which you have called and those in which you have just been a participant? _____

   c. Describe the last time you put your "**foot in your mouth**". _____

9. WRITTEN COMMUNICATION

   a. How would you describe your **writing style** in comparison with others' styles? _____

   b. Describe your **approach to writing**—do you "write" in your head and dictate a final copy, go through many editing stages, or what? _____

10. EDUCATION (Covered in Education section)

11. EXPERIENCE/KNOWLEDGE (Covered in Work History, although any doubts about level of knowledge should be resolved. Devise your own line of questions to "**calibrate**" the individual's level of expertise. Determine exactly what sorts of **organization climates** (formal/informal, fast-changing/stagnant, growing/declining) the person has worked in and prefers.)

PERSONAL CHARACTERISTICS

12. MOTIVATION/DRIVE

   *a. What **motivates** you? _____

   *b. How many **hours per week** have you worked, on the average, during the past year? _____

   *c. Describe the **pace** at which you work—fast, slow, or moderate—and the circumstances under which it varies.

   d. Who have been your major **career influences,** and why? _____

13. INITIATIVE, A "DOER"

   a. What are examples of circumstances in which you were expected to do a certain thing and, on your own, went beyond the **call of duty**? _____

   b. Are you better at **initiating** a lot of things or hammering out results for fewer things? _____

   c. In what specific ways have you **changed an organization** the most (in terms of direction, results, policies)?

14. EXCELLENCE STANDARDS (Covered in Work History)

15. ORGANIZATION/PLANNING

   *a. How would you describe your **work habits**? _____

   *b. How well **organized** are you; what do you do to be organized and what, if anything, do you feel you ought to do to be better organized? _____

   c. Describe a situation that did **not go as well** as planned. What would you have done differently? _____

16. INDEPENDENCE
    a. How much **supervision** do you want or need? _____
    _____

17. "TRACK RECORD"
    a. What are the most important **lessons** you have learned in your career (get specifics with respect to when, where, what, etc.)? _____
    _____

18. EMOTIONAL STABILITY
    *a. How do you handle yourself under **stress** and pressure? _____
    _____

    *b. Describe yourself in terms of **emotional control**; what sorts of things irritate you the most or get you down?
    _____
    _____

    *c. How many times have you "**lost your cool**" in the past couple of months? _____

    *d. What sort of **mood swings** do you experience—how high are the highs, how low are the lows, and why?
    _____
    _____

    e. Describe a situation in which your emotional **controls** were **inadequate**. _____
    _____

    f. Describe a situation in which you were the **most angry** you have been in years. _____
    _____

    g. What have been the most difficult **criticisms** for you to accept? _____
    _____

19. SELF-OBJECTIVITY
    a. What are your principal **developmental needs** and what are plans to deal with them? _____
    _____

20. ADAPTABILITY
    *a. How have you **changed** during recent years? _____
    _____

    *b. What sorts of **organization changes** have you found easiest and most difficult to accept? _____
    _____

    c. What changes in your **approach** would be most appropriate in your next job? _____
    _____

    d. What actions would you take in the **first week**, should you join our organization? _____
    _____

21. PERSONAL INTEGRITY
    a. Describe a situation or two in which the pressures to **compromise your integrity** were the strongest you have ever felt.
    _____

INTERPERSONAL RELATIONS

22. FIRST IMPRESSION (Evaluated directly by interviewer)

23. ENTHUSIASM
    a. How would you rate yourself (and why) in **enthusiasm** and charisma? _____
    _____

24. LIKABILITY
    a. Tell me about a situation in which you were expected to work with a person you **disliked**. _____
    _____

25. EMPATHY/LISTENING (Determined in other sections of Guide and by direct observation by interviewer)

26. ASSERTIVENESS
   a. How would you describe your level of **assertiveness**? _____
   _____

   *b. Please give a couple of recent specific examples in which you were **highly assertive**—one in which the outcome was favorable and one where it wasn't. _____
   _____
   _____

27. NEGOTIATION SKILLS
   a. Describe situations in which your **negotiation skills** proved effective and ineffective. _____
   _____

   *b. Describe a situation in which you were most effective **selling** an idea or yourself. _____
   _____

28. TEAM PLAYER
   a. What will reference checks disclose to be the common perception among **peers** regarding how much of a **team player** you are? _____
   _____

   b. Describe the most **difficult person** with whom you have had to work. _____
   _____

   c. Tell me about a situation in which you felt **others were wrong** and you were right. _____
   _____

29. CLIENT NEEDS DIAGNOSIS
   a. Describe your methods of **diagnosing client needs**. _____
   _____

30. POLITICAL SAVVY
   *a. How aware are you of **political forces** that may affect your performance? Please give a couple of examples of the most difficult political situations in which you have been involved. _____
   _____

LEADERSHIP/MANAGEMENT
(Questions 31-39 are dealt with in Work History and Management sections.)

ADDITIONAL PERSON SPECIFICATIONS

40. AMBITION (Dealt with in Plans and Goals section)

41. RISK TAKING
   *a. What are the biggest **risks** you have taken in recent years? _____
   _____

42. COMPATIBILITY OF INTERESTS WITH THIS ORGANIZATION
   a. Is there anything we or I can do to **help you** if there is a job change (relocation, housing, schools)?
   _____
   _____

43. HEALTH
   a. Do you have any **health problems** which might interfere with your ability to do the job? _____
   _____

44. BALANCE IN LIFE
   a. How satisfied are you with your **balance in life**—the balance among work, wellness, family, community involvement, professional associations, friendships, hobbies, and interests? _____
   _____

SUMMARY

RATING SCALE: 4 = Excellent, 3 = Good, 2 = Only Fair, 1 = Poor, 0 = Very Poor

Person Specification	Base Rating*	Your Rating	Comments
1. Learning Ability			
2. Analysis Skills			
3. Judgment			
4. Conceptual Skill			
5. Creativity/Innovativeness			
6. Strategic Planning			
7. Pragmatism			
8. Oral Communications			
9. Written Communications			
10. Education			
11. Experience/Knowledge			
12. Motivation/Drive			
13. Initiative; a "Doer"			
14. Excellence Standards			
15. Organization/Planning			
16. Independence			
17. "Track Record"			
18. Emotional Stability			
19. Self-Objectivity			
20. Adaptability			
21. Personal Integrity			
22. First Impression			
23. Enthusiasm			
24. Likability			
25. Empathy/Listening			

*Base Rating is minimally acceptable rating for the person to be hired/promoted.

Person Specification	Base Rating	Your Rating	Comments
26. Assertiveness			
27. Negotiation Skills			
28. Team Player			
29. Client Need Diagnosis			
30. Political Savvy			
31. Leadership			
32. Recruitment			
33. Training/Development			
34. Goal Setting			
35. Delegation			
36. Monitoring Performance			
37. Performance Feedback			
38. Removing Non-Performers			
39. Team Development			

ADDITIONAL PERSON SPECIFICATIONS

	Base Rating	Your Rating	Comments
40. Ambition			
41. Risk-Taking			
42. Compatibility of Interests with this Organization			
43. Health			
44. Balance in Life			

B Person Specifications

The general person specifications listed in Appendix B1 correspond to the 44 person specifications listed in the last two pages of the In-Depth Selection Interview Guide.

Placed on a word processor, it is easy to modify definitions to fit the particular job you are filling. Keep the person specs that apply, discard those that don't, and add any that your job analysis mandates. Then establish the base rating (minimum rating acceptable to be offered the job). The base ratings should be entered on the last two pages of the Guide.

Appendices B2 through B6 are examples of person specifications modified for specific jobs, with base ratings stated.

GENERAL PERSON SPECIFICATIONS

Intellectual Characteristics

1. *Learning Ability:* Demonstrates ability to acquire understanding quickly and absorb new information rapidly. This person specification reflects neither motivation to learn nor willingness to accept change; rather, it reflects the intellectual *capacity* that, when combined with motivation, will result in learning.

2. *Analysis Skill:* Identifies significant problems. Analyzes problem situations in depth. Gathers facts and opinions, determines root causes, and determines subtle relationships among important factors. Demonstrates a probing mind.

3. *Judgment:* Demonstrates consistent logic, rationality, and objectivity in decision making. Achieves optimum balance between quick decisiveness and slower, more systematic approaches; i.e., is neither indecisive nor a hip-shooter. Shows common sense. Anticipates consequences of actions.

4. *Conceptual Skill:* Deals effectively not just with concrete, tangible issues, but with abstract, conceptual matters.

5. *Creativity/Innovativeness:* Generates new (creative) approaches to problems or original modifications (innovations) to established approaches. Shows imagination and vision.

6. *Strategic Planning:* Determines opportunities and threats through comprehensive analysis of current and future trends. Accurately assesses own organization's competitive strengths and vulnerabilities. Makes tactical and strategic adjustments incorporating new data. Comprehends the "big picture."

7. *Pragmatism:* Generates sensible, realistic, practical solutions to problems.

8. *Oral Communications:* Communicates effectively one to one, in small groups and in public speaking contexts. Demonstrates fluency, "quickness on one's feet," clarity, organization of thought processes, and command of the language.

9. *Written Communications:* Writes clear, precise, well-organized memos, letters and proposals while using appropriate vocabulary, grammar, and word usage, and creating the appropriate "flavor."

10. *Education:* (Requisite level will depend on job analysis.)

11. *Experience/Knowledge:* (_____) years of experience (specify). Remains current through readings, courses, seminars, network, and professional organizations.

Personal Characteristics

12. *Motivation/Drive:* Exhibits energy, strong desire to achieve, appropriately high dedication level. Although hours per se are less important than results, (_____) hours or more per week are probably necessary for results expected.

13. *Initiative:* A "doer." Does not just talk, but follows through aggressively to successful completion. Action-oriented and results-oriented. Actively seeks out opportunities to make a contribution rather than simply "get by" with what is expected. Shows perseverance—the capacity to "hang in there" to successful completion.

14. *Excellence Standards:* Strives for and consistently achieves quality results—demonstrates low tolerance for mediocrity. Maintains high standards of performance. Exhibits conscientiousness, dedication, self-discipline, and a sense of responsibility.

15. *Organization/Planning:* Plans, organizes, schedules, prioritizes, and budgets in an efficient, productive manner. Utilizes time efficiently. Effectively juggles several projects. Shows consistent reliability.

16. *Independence:* Functions successfully without much supervision.

17. *"Track Record":* Has successful career history. Repeated failures with "good excuses" probably not acceptable. Recent track record weighed heavily.

18. *Emotional Stability:* Under pressure from competition, time scarcity, personal problems, requirements by supervisors, or other sources, retains emotional control, honesty, and productivity. Does not make "flighty" decisions nor excessively "lose one's cool." Exhibits a positive self-concept and generally positive outlook on life. Able to "take rejection" while maintaining effectiveness.

19. *Self-Objectivity:* Recognizes not just one's own strengths but also shortcomings and areas for improvement. Demonstrates the courage not to be defensive, rationalize mistakes, blame others for one's own failures. Builds feedback mechanisms to minimize "blind spots."

    Note: High self-objectivity is necessary, but not sufficient for a person to be adaptable and self-correcting.

20. *Adaptability:* Converts self-objectivity into self-correction and personal improvement. Actively supports necessary organization change. Not rigid—intellectually, emotionally, interpersonally. Adjusts quickly to changing priorities. Copes effectively with complexity.

21. *Personal Integrity:* Remains consistent in terms of what one says and does and in terms of behavior toward others. Earns trust of co-workers by maintaining confidences. Does what is right, not what is politically expedient. "Fights fair."

Interpersonal Relations

22. *First Impression:* Creates favorable first impression through acceptable attire, body structure, grooming, voice qualities, eye contact, gestures, personal hygiene, and bearing.

23. *Enthusiasm:* Exhibits charisma, dynamism, and excitement.

24. *Likability:* Wins the liking and respect of people. Demonstrates interpersonal flexibility, friendliness, sense of humor, and genuineness. Exhibits warmth and caring. Shows tact and diplomacy.

25. *Empathy/Listening:* "Tunes in" accurately to the feelings, moods, needs, and attitudes of others. Understands the impact of one's behavior on others. Demonstrates good listening skills.

26. *Assertiveness:* Takes forceful stands on issues, without being excessively abrasive.

27. *Negotiation Skills:* Identifies conflict (vs. problem-solving) situations. Determines opponent's negotiating strengths and vulnerabilities. Achieves maximum "win" combined with appropriate satisfaction by opponent.

28. *Team Player:* Cooperates with supervisors (without being a "yes person"), and establishes cohesive, effective, collaborative relationships with peers (without being a "pushover").

29. *Client Need Diagnosis:* Quickly and accurately determines client (internal or external) needs.

30. *Political Savvy:* Shows awareness of political factors and "hidden agendas," and behaves shrewdly without being a self-seeking "back-stabber." Recognizes where to go to get things done and builds informal network to "wire" information sources and influence.

Leadership/Management

31. *Leadership:* Persuades and inspires people to follow, whether through quiet substance, charismatic excitement, or some blend of both.

32. *Recruitment:* Achieves record of success in recruiting, interviewing, and hiring people. Has low percentage of mishires.

33. *Training and Development:* Actively and successfully trains people for current assignments and develops them for promotion into positions in which they succeed.

34. *Goal Setting:* Sets clear, fair, challenging goals with subordinates, encouraging appropriate individual initiative.

35. *Delegation:* Delegates appropriate responsibility, with sufficient authority and resources.

36. *Monitoring Performance:* Knows what subordinates are doing in sufficient depth to "spot" emerging problems early, yet not "over-supervise."

37. *Performance Feedback:* Provides clear, thorough, positive (praise and recognition) performance feedback on a day-to-day basis, within the context of high performance standards; thoroughly and sensitively

provides constructive criticism. Produces "no surprises" in annual performance appraisals.

38. *Removing Non-Performers:* Demonstrates a willingness to remove (demote, transfer, or terminate) employees who have demonstrated an inability to achieve mutually acceptable standards of performance in a reasonable time frame, following reasonable attempts to develop the individual.

39. *Team Development:* Achieves cohesive, effective (positive, mutually supportive) "team spirit" with subordinates. Team "climate" characterized by open, honest relationships in which differences are constructively resolved rather than ignored, suppressed or denied.

Additional Person Specifications

40. *Ambition:* Demonstrates a desire to move upward in the organization.

41. *Risk-taking:* Demonstrates willingness to take a calculated risk without "betting the farm."

42. *Compatibility of Interests with This Organization:* Demonstrates needs (for money, recognition, affiliation, achievement, prestige, promotion, power, location, amount and type of travel, or whatever) consistent with the opportunities available in the foreseeable future.

43. *Health:* Physical age equal to or less than chronological age. Maintains weight, diet, and alcohol use within normal range. Exercises regularly. Has no health problems that might seriously affect attendance or productivity.

    Note: Medical evaluation should be performed by a physician.

44. *Balance in Life:* Achieves sufficient balance among work, wellness, family, community involvement, professional associations, friendships, hobbies, and interests. "Sufficient" may be defined variously, reflecting necessity of meeting current work challenges, the possibility of "burn out," or the consequences of sacrificing so much currently that later in life there are severe regrets.

Appendix B2

The General Manager person specifications are broadly applicable. That is, by changing only a few words in the definition, and of course by changing base ratings, these specs "fit" for general managers of a tiny manufacturing company or CEO of a major financial institution.

GENERAL MANAGER (CEO) PERSON SPECIFICATIONS

Intellectual Characteristics

1. *Learning Ability:* Demonstrates ability to acquire understanding quickly and absorb new information rapidly. This person specification reflects neither motivation to learn nor willingness to accept change; rather it reflects the intellectual *capacity* that, when combined with motivation, will result in learning.

2. *Analytic Skill:* Identifies significant problems. Analyses problem situations in depth. Gathers facts and opinions, determines root causes, and determines subtle relationships among important factors. Demonstrates a probing mind.

3. *Judgment:* Demonstrates consistent logic, rationality, and objectivity in decision making. Achieves optimum balance between quick decisiveness and slower, more systematic approaches; i.e., is neither indecisive nor a hip-shooter. Shows common sense. Anticipates consequences of actions.

4. *Conceptual Skill:* Deals effectively not just with concrete, tangible issues, but with abstract, conceptual matters.

5. *Creativity/Innovativeness:* Generates new (creative) approaches to problems or original modifications (innovations) to established approaches. Shows imagination and vision.

6. *Strategic Planning:* Determines opportunities and threats through comprehensive analysis of current and future trends. Accurately assesses own organization's competitive strengths and vulnerabilities. Makes tactical and strategic adjustments incorporating new data. Comprehends the "big picture."

7. *Pragmatism:* Generates sensible, realistic, practical solutions to problems.

8. *Oral Communications:* Communicates effectively one to one, in small groups and in public speaking contexts. Demonstrates fluency, "quickness on one's feet," clarity, organization of thought processes, and command of the language.

9. *Written Communications:* Writes clear, precise, well-organized memos, letters and proposals while using appropriate vocabulary, grammar, and word usage, and creating the appropriate "flavor."

10. *Education:* MBA or equivalent.

11. *Experience/Knowledge:* Executive responsibility for minimum two of the following: operations, marketing, engineering, sales, administration, with 10 years of experience total. Remains current through readings, courses, seminars, network, and professional organizations.

Personal Characteristics

12. *Motivation/Drive:* Exhibits energy, strong desire to achieve, appropriately high dedication level. Although hours per se are less important than results, 55 hours or more per week are probably necessary for results expected.

13. *Initiative, a "Doer":* Does not just talk, but follows through aggressively to successful completion. Action-oriented and results-oriented. Actively seeks out opportunities to make a contribution rather than simply "get by" with what is expected. Shows perseverance—the capacity to "hang in there" to successful completion.

14. *Excellence Standards:* Strives for and consistently achieves quality results—demonstrates low tolerance for mediocrity. Maintains high

standards of performance. Exhibits conscientiousness, dedication, self-discipline, and a sense of responsibility.

15. *Organization/Planning:* Plans, organizes, schedules, prioritizes, and budgets in an efficient, productive manner. Utilizes time efficiently. Effectively juggles several projects. Shows consistent reliability and self-discipline.

16. *Independence:* Functions successfully without much supervision.

17. *"Track Record":* Has successful career history. Repeated failures with "good excuses" probably not acceptable. Recent track record weighed heavily.

18. *Emotional Stability:* Under pressure from competition, time scarcity, personal problems, requirements by supervisors, or other sources, retains emotional control, honesty, and productivity. Does not make "flighty" decisions nor excessively "lose one's cool." Exhibits a positive self-concept and generally positive outlook on life. Able to "take rejection" while maintaining effectiveness.

19. *Self-Objectivity:* Recognizes not just one's own strengths but also shortcomings and areas for improvement. Demonstrates the courage not to be defensive, rationalize mistakes, nor blame others for one's own failures. Builds feedback mechanisms to minimize "blind spots."

    Note: High self-objectivity is necessary, but not sufficient for a person to be adaptable and self-correcting.

20. *Adaptability:* Converts high self-objectivity into self-correction and personal improvement. Actively supports necessary organization change. Not rigid—intellectually, emotionally, nor interpersonally. Adjusts quickly to changing priorities. Copes effectively with complexity.

21. *Personal Integrity:* Remains consistent in terms of what one says and does and in terms of behavior toward others. Earns trust of co-workers by maintaining confidences. Does what is right, not what is politically expedient. "Fights fair."

Interpersonal Relations

22. *First Impression:* Creates favorable first impression through acceptable attire, body structure, grooming, voice qualities, eye contact, gestures, personal hygiene, and bearing.

23. *Enthusiasm:* Exhibits charisma, dynamism, and excitement.

24. *Likability:* Wins the liking and respect of people. Demonstrates interpersonal flexibility, friendliness, sense of humor, and genuineness. Exhibits warmth and caring. Shows tact and diplomacy.

25. *Empathy/Listening:* "Tunes in" accurately to the feelings, moods, needs, and attitudes of others. Understands the impact of one's behavior on others. Demonstrates good listening skills.

26. *Assertiveness:* Takes forceful stands on issues, without being excessively abrasive.

27. *Negotiation Skills:* Identifies conflict (vs. problem-solving) situations. Determines opponent's negotiating strengths and vulnerabilities. Achieves maximum "win" combined with appropriate satisfaction by opponent.

28. *Team Player:* Cooperates with supervisors (without being a "yes person"), and establishes cohesive, effective, collaborative relationships with peers (without being a "push-over").

29. *Client Need Diagnosis:* Quickly and accurately determines client (internal or external) needs.

30. *Political Savvy:* Shows awareness of political factors and "hidden agendas," and behaves shrewdly without being a self-seeking "back-stabber." Recognizes where to go to get things done and builds informal network to "wire" information sources and influence.

Leadership/Management

31. *Leadership:* Persuades and inspires people to follow, whether through quiet substance, charismatic excitement, or some blend of both.

32. *Recruitment:* Achieves record of success in recruiting, interviewing, and hiring people. Has low percentage of "mishires."

33. *Training and Development:* Actively and successfully trains people for current assignments and develops them for promotion into positions in which they succeed.

34. *Goal Setting:* Sets clear, fair, challenging goals with subordinates, encouraging appropriate individual initiative.

35. *Delegation:* Delegates appropriate responsibility, with sufficient authority and resources.

36. *Monitoring Performance:* Knows what subordinates are doing in sufficient depth to "spot" emerging problems early, yet not "over-supervise."

37. *Performance Feedback:* Provides clear, thorough, positive (praise and recognition) performance feedback on a day-to-day basis, within the context of high performance standards; thoroughly and sensitively provides constructive criticism. Produces "no surprises" in annual performance appraisals.

38. *Removing Non-Performers:* Demonstrates willingness to remove (demote, transfer, or terminate) employees who have demonstrated an inability to achieve mutually acceptable standards of performance in a reasonable time frame, following reasonable attempts to develop the individual.

39. *Team Development:* Achieves cohesive, effective (positive, mutually supportive) "team spirit" with subordinates. Team "climate" characterized by open, honest relationships in which differences are constructively resolved rather than ignored, suppressed, or denied.

Additional Person Specifications

40. *Ambition:* Demonstrates a desire to move upward in the organization.

41. *Risk-taking:* Demonstrates willingness to take a calculated risk without "betting the farm."

42. *Compatibility of Interests with This Organization:* Demonstrates needs (for money, recognition, affiliation, achievement, prestige, promotion, power, location, amount and type of travel, or whatever) consistent with the opportunities available in the foreseeable future.

43. *Health:* Physical age equal to or less than chronological age. Maintains weight, diet, and alcohol use within normal range. Exercises regularly. Has no health problems that might seriously affect attendance or productivity.

    Note: Medical evaluation to be performed by a physician.

44. *Balance in Life:* Achieves sufficient balance among work, wellness, family, community involvement, professional associations, friendships, hobbies, and interests. "Sufficient" may be defined variously, reflecting necessity of meeting current work challenges, the possibility of "burn out," or the consequences of sacrificing so much currently that later in life there are severe regrets.

PERSON SPECIFICATIONS FOR TECHNICAL PROFESSIONAL

The following Technical Professional person specifications were devised from dozens of different descriptions of technical professional jobs. The base ratings are to be created by the hiring manager; the base ratings given here serve only as a sample.

Scale: 4 = Excellent 2 = Only Fair 3 = Good 1 = Poor	Base Rating	Your Rating
1. *Judgment:* Learns quickly. Makes decisions in a logical, rational manner. Demonstrates appropriate balance between quick, intuitive decisiveness and slower, more thorough, systematic problem-solving. Shows "common sense."	3+	
2. *Analytic Ability:* Analyzes problems in depth. Gathers facts, determines causes and breaks down problems into components. Demonstrates a probing mind.	4	
3. *Creativity:* Generates new approaches to some problems or original modifications to established approaches. Demonstrates imagination and vision.	3	
4. *Pragmatism:* Generates sensible, realistic, practical solutions to problems.	3	
5. *Intellectual Flexibility:* Effectively juggles several projects simultaneously. Thinks concretely as well as abstractly. Deals effectively with complexity and diversity.	3+	

	Base Rating	Your Rating
6. *Oral Communications:* Communicates effectively one to one and in small groups. Demonstrates fluency, clarity, organization of thought processes, conciseness, and the ability to respond effectively to direct questions.	3	
7. *Written Communications:* Writes clear, precise, well-organized proposals and reports using appropriate vocabulary, grammar, and word usage, and creating the appropriate "flavor."	3+	
8. *Education:* Must demonstrate ability to handle diverse subjects in an above average manner by maintaining a strong B GPA in formal coursework. Bachelor degree minimum level, graduate degree preferred.	3+	
9. *Experience:* Technical experience germane to the job at hand, preferably in a semi-structured environment, with verifiable successes. 5-10 years of relevant experience expected.	3	
10. *Initiative, a "Doer":* Does not just talk, but follows through efficiently and productively. Action-oriented and results-oriented. Actively seeks out opportunities to make a contribution rather than simply "getting by" with what is expected.	4	
11. *Self-Objectivity:* Demonstrates accurate self-insights, with respect to not just strengths, but also shortcomings and areas for improvement. Does not excessively rationalize or blame others for mistakes and failures.	3	
12. *Perseverance:* "Hangs in there" to successful completion, despite obstacles.	3	
13. *Independence:* Functions successfully without much supervision.	4	

	Base Rating	Your Rating
14. *Standards of Performance:* Strives for and consistently achieves quality results; demonstrates low tolerance for mediocrity. Exhibits conscientiousness, dedication, self-discipline, and responsibility.	4	
15. *"Track Record":* Has successful career history. Repeated failures with "good excuses" probably not acceptable. Recent track record is weighed most heavily.	3	
16. *Emotional Stability:* Under pressure from competition, time scarcity, personal problems, requirements by supervisors or other factors, retains emotional control, honesty, and productivity. Does not make "flighty" decisions or excessively "lose one's cool." Exhibits a positive self-concept. Able to "take rejection" while maintaining effectiveness.	3	
17. *Organization/Planning:* Plans, organizes, schedules, budgets, coordinates, and sorts out priorities in such a way as to achieve timely results. Manages time efficiently. Shows sufficient detail orientation.	3	
18. *First Impression:* Creates favorable first impression through acceptable attire, grooming, voice qualities, eye contact, gestures, personal hygiene, and bearing.	2	
19. *Likability:* Wins liking and respect of people. Demonstrates flexibility, friendliness, and honesty in dealing with people.	2	
20. *Assertiveness:* Takes forceful stands on issues, without being excessively abrasive.	2	

	Base Rating	Your Rating

21. *Team Player:* Cooperates with supervisors (without being a "yes person"), and establishes cohesive, effective, collaborative relationships with peers (without being a "pushover"). Although the person may be a solitary performer much of the time, at some point it is important to communicate effectively with co-workers. — **3+**

22. *Enthusiasm:* Exhibits charisma, dynamism, excitement, and persuasiveness. — **2**

23. *Empathy/Listening:* "Tunes in" accurately to the feelings, needs, and attitudes of others; understands the impact of one's own behavior on others; demonstrates good listening skills. — **2+**

24. *Motivation/Drive:* Exhibits energy, strong desire to achieve, and an appropriately high dedication level. Although hours per se are less important than results, occasionally extremely long hours are necessary. — **3**

25. *Health:* Physical age equal to or less than chronological age. Maintains weight, diet, and alcohol use within normal range. Exercises regularly. Has no health problems that might seriously affect attendance or productivity. — **2**

26. *Ambition:* Demonstrates desire to progress to sales management. — **2**

27. *Compatibility of Interests with the Company:* Demonstrates needs (for money, recognition, affiliation, achievement, prestige, promotion, power, location, amount and type of travel, or whatever) consistent with the opportunities available in the foreseeable future. — **3**

28. *Leadership:* Inspires people to follow. — **2**

	Base Rating	Your Rating
29. *Recruitment:* Achieves record of success in recruiting, interviewing, and hiring people. Has low percentage of "mishires."	N/A	
30. *Training:* Actively and successfully trains people for current assignments and develops them for promotion into positions in which they succeed.	N/A	
31. *Goal Setting:* Sets clear, fair, challenging goals with subordinates, using management by objectives or comparable approach.	N/A	
32. *Delegation:* Delegates appropriate responsibility and authority.	N/A	
33. *Monitoring Performance:* Knows what subordinates are doing in sufficient depth to "spot" emerging problems early, yet not "over-supervise."	N/A	
34. *Performance Feedback:* Provides clear, positive (praise and recognition), thorough, performance feedback on a day-to-day basis, within the context of high performance standards; thoroughly and sensitively provides constructive criticism. Produces "no surprises" in annual performance appraisals.	N/A	
35. *Removing Non-Performance:* Demonstrates willingness to remove (demote, transfer, or terminate) employees who have shown an inability to achieve mutually acceptable standards of performance in a reasonable time-frame, following reasonable attempts to develop the individual.	N/A	

	Base Rating	Your Rating
36. *Team Development:* Achieves cohesive, effective (positive, mutually supportive) "team spirit" with subordinates. Team "climate" characterized by open, honest, mutually supportive communications and relationships in which differences are constructively resolved rather than ignored, suppressed, or denied.	N/A	

Additional Person Specifications

	Base Rating	Your Rating
37. *Political Savvy:* Shows awareness of political factors and "hidden agendas," and behaves shrewdly without being a self-seeking "back-stabber."	2	
38. *Policy Adherence:* Shows awareness of policies and procedures, conforms to them willingly, yet acts to alter distasteful policies/procedures while working "through the system."	2+	
39. *Adaptability:* Able to cope (intellectually, personally, and interpersonally) with a changing environment.	3+	

Appendix B4

PERSON SPECIFICATIONS FOR MANAGER TECHNICAL SERVICES

The Manager Technical Services person specifications have an accompanying job description. Both are "real examples," with company name omitted. The base ratings are actual, as determined by the hiring manager and human resources professional. Naturally, a job with the same title in a different company might have some different person specifications and different base ratings.

Scale:	4 = Excellent 3 = Good	2 = Only Fair 1 = Poor	Base Rating	Your Rating
1. *Analytic Skill:* Analyzes problems in depth. Achieves satisfactory results on PAT and PI. (4) would represent exceptional PAT or PI performance.			4	
2. *Judgment:* Learns quickly. Stays abreast of industry technology. Demonstrates proficiency in at least one approved programming language or capacity to quickly develop it. Logical thinker. Shows "common sense." (4) level would represent current proficiency in more than one approved programming language, capacity for higher-level decision making, or extraordinary ability to learn quickly.			4	

	Base Rating	Your Rating
3. *Creativity:* Generates new approaches to problems or original modifications to established approaches. Demonstrates imagination and vision. Shows ability to lead a marketing group into the future by promoting marketing requirements and developing innovative products.	4	
4. *Pragmatism:* Generates sensible, realistic, practical solutions to problems. Shows ability to justify, on practical business grounds, recommendations for updating outdated systems, technology, and procedures.	4	
5. *Intellectual Flexibility:* Effectively juggles several projects simultaneously. Thinks concretely as well as abstractly. Deals effectively with complexity and diversity in both technical and business matters. Demonstrates ability to juggle current and future projects in hardware, software, and applications.	4	
6. *Oral Communications:* Communicates effectively one to one, in small groups, and in public speaking contexts. Demonstrates fluency, "quickness on one's feet," clarity, organization of thought processes, and command of the language. (4) would constitute exceptional effectiveness in "selling" concepts.	3	
7. *Written Communications:* Writes clear, precise, well-organized memos, letters, and proposals while using appropriate vocabulary, grammar, and word usage, and creating the appropriate "flavor." (4) would represent exceptional written communications.	3	

	Base Rating	Your Rating

8. *Education:* BS degree in computer science, mathematics, or business administration. (4) would represent accredited graduate degree in one of the above areas. — **3**

9. *Experience:* Ten years practical experience in data processing environment and systems programming. Must be familiar with IBM, Tandem, and HP hardware, have VM knowledge and experience, and have solid knowledge of CICS, VTAM, PC, VSAM, and teleprocessing or database software. (4) would include above plus accounting/ financial knowledge at a graduate level. — **3**

10. *Initiative, a "Doer":* Does not just talk, but follows through efficiently and productively. Action-oriented and results-oriented. Actively seeks out opportunities to make a contribution rather than simply "getting by" with what is expected. — **4**

11. *Self-Objectivity:* Demonstrates accurate self-insights, with respect to not just strengths, but also shortcomings and areas for improvement. Does not excessively rationalize or blame others for mistakes and failures. — **3**

12. *Perseverance:* "Hangs in there" to successful completion, despite obstacles. — **4**

13. *Independence:* Functions successfully without much supervision. — **4**

14. *Standards of Performance:* Strives for and consistently achieves quality results; demonstrates low tolerance for mediocrity. Exhibits conscientiousness, dedication, self-discipline, and responsibility. — **4**

	Base Rating	Your Rating
15. *"Track Record":* Has successful career history. Repeated failures with "good excuses" probably not acceptable. Recent track record is weighed most heavily.	3	
16. *Emotional Stability:* Under pressure from competition, time scarcity, personal problems, requirements by supervisors or other factors, retains emotional control, honesty, and productivity. Does not make "flighty" decisions or excessively "lose one's cool." Exhibits a positive self-concept. Able to "take rejection" while maintaining effectiveness.	3	
17. *Organization/Planning:* Plans, organizes, schedules, budgets, coordinates, and sorts out priorities in such a way as to achieve timely results. Manages time efficiently. Shows sufficient detail orientation.	4	
18. *First Impression:* Creates favorable first impression through acceptable attire, grooming, voice qualities, eye contact, gestures, personal hygiene, and bearing.	3	
19. *Likability:* Wins liking and respect of people. Demonstrates flexibility, friendliness, and honesty in dealing with people.	3	
20. *Assertiveness:* Takes forceful stands on issues, without being excessively abrasive. A (4) is undesirable.	3	
21. *Team Player:* Cooperates with supervisors (without being a "yes person"), and establishes cohesive, effective, collaborative relationships with peers (without being a "pushover").	3	

	Base Rating	Your Rating

22. *Enthusiasm:* Exhibits charisma, dynamism, excitement, and persuasiveness. Demonstrates ability to persuade without having line authority over people. — **3**

23. *Empathy/Listening:* "Tunes in" accurately to the feelings, needs, and attitudes of others; understands the impact of one's own behavior on others; demonstrates good listening skills. — **3**

24. *Motivation/Drive:* Exhibits energy, strong desire to achieve, and an appropriately high dedication level. Although hours per se are less important than results, 48 hours or more per week are reasonably expected. — **3**

25. *Health:* Physical age equal to or less than chronological age. Maintains weight, diet, and alcohol use within normal range. Exercises regularly. Has no health problems that might seriously affect attendance or productivity. — **3**

26. *Ambition:* Demonstrates desire to move upward in the organizational hierarchy. With 29% of those leaving the company in 1985 stating the reason as "lack of career growth," a *moderate* desire to move ahead is most desirable. A (4), or extremely high desire to move up rapidly, perhaps more rapidly than the company can accommodate, would represent a mismatch. — **3**

27. *Compatibility of Interests with the Company:* Demonstrates needs (for money, recognition, affiliation, achievement, prestige, promotion, power, location, amount and type of travel, or whatever) consistent with the opportunities available in the foreseeable future. — **4**

28. *Leadership:* Inspires people to follow. — **3**

	Base Rating	Your Rating
29. *Recruitment:* Achieves record of success in recruiting, interviewing, and hiring people. Has low percentage of "mishires."	3	
30. *Training:* Actively and successfully trains people for current assignments and develops them for promotion into positions in which they succeed.	3	
31. *Goal Setting:* Sets clear, fair, challenging goals with subordinates, using management by objectives or comparable approach.	3	
32. *Delegation:* Delegates appropriate responsibility and authority.	3	
33. *Monitoring Performance:* Knows what subordinates are doing in sufficient depth to "spot" emerging problems early, yet not "over-supervise."	3	
34. *Performance Feedback:* Provides clear, positive (praise and recognition), thorough, performance feedback on a day-to-day basis, within the context of high performance standards; thoroughly and sensitively provides constructive criticism. Produces "no surprises" in annual performance appraisals.	3	
35. *Removing Non-Performers:* Demonstrates willingness to remove (demote, transfer, or terminate) employees who have shown an inability to achieve mutually acceptable standards of performance in a reasonable time-frame, following reasonable attempts to develop the individual.	3	

	Base Rating	Your Rating
36. *Team Development:* Achieves cohesive, effective (positive, mutually supportive) "team spirit" with subordinates. Team "climate" characterized by open, honest, mutually supportive communications and relationships in which differences are constructively resolved rather than ignored, suppressed, or denied.	3	

Additional Person Specifications

37. *Political Savvy:* Shows awareness of political factors and "hidden agendas," and behaves shrewdly without being a self-seeking "back-stabber."	3	
38. *Policy Adherence:* Shows awareness of policies and procedures, conforms to them willingly, yet acts to alter distasteful policies/procedures while working "through the system."	3	

JOB DESCRIPTION—MANAGER, TECHNICAL SERVICES

Computer Services Company

> *Job Title:* Manager, Technical Services
>
> *Reports to:* Director Operations and Systems

The Nature and Scope of the Position

The Manager of Technical Services is responsible for delivery of technical direction of the Financial Services Group and ensuring that hardware, software, and applications within the group are properly installed and supported. This incorporates hardware and software planning and implementations as well as complete Network Management of all communications responsibilities within the group. The major role is to keep the company abreast of industry technology and standards, and ensure we have the proper delivery systems in place to launch the group's new products and services.

Main Responsibilities

1. Manage all software implementations ensuring high quality development work, meeting all target dates and offering a smooth transition into the production environment, including training, policies and procedures, and implementation support.

2. Prepare corporate business cases to justify the purchase of all new hardware. This includes new products and replacement of existing machinery.

3. Manage the installation or replacement of new hardware ensuring there is no degradation to service during the transition. Installation plans, proper training procedures, and installation support must be provided by the team.

4. Research, recommend, and implement new vehicles for communication and network management linking IBM, Tandem, and eventually the company network to accommodate and link all Financial Services Group.

5. Lead Marketing Services into the future by promoting market requirements and develop products to fulfill these requirements and technology advancements.

6. Interact with Systems Development coordinating project plans, utilizing development and implementation techniques for software products.

7. Promote technical leadership offering recommendations for updating outdated systems, techniques, and procedures. Justify reasons, advantages, and disadvantages for updating technology to industry standards.

8. Prepare equipment capacity planning tools evaluating hardware performance, software, and communication capacity. Continual monitoring of reports providing system integrity guarantees, and ensuring capacity coincides with forecasts and marketing requirements.

General Responsibilities

1. Ensure the group is provided proper technological leadership in the planning, installation, and support of hardware, software applications and services.

2. To manage and motivate subordinates through regular meetings and one-to-one interfacing.

3. To complete performance reviews for each subordinate including motivations, objectives, and recommendations for educational improvements.

4. To perform regular staff and environmental resource analysis, and ensure that maximum efficiency is being maintained.

5. To plan the future direction and objectives of the department.

6. Preparation of business cases to justify personnel or equipment requirements, and to be involved in the acquisition of those requirements.

7. The analysis of all statistical reports produced by the department to ensure that the best possible standards are being attained in a cost-effective manner.

8. The preparation of a departmental five-year plan to be used in conjunction with other areas to produce an overall Production Services five-year plan.

9. To establish an annual budget, and to be prepared to reconcile any differences between forecasts and actuals.

10. To remain current with all technical and market changes that may affect the performance of the area.

11. To effectively promote the image of the Production Services department.

12. To establish a good working relationship with all areas of Production Services as well as with other departments, external users, and suppliers.

13. To control and to allocate resources for the implementation of new projects without impacting the regular functions of the area.

Education

Bachelor of Science in Computer Science, Mathematics or Business Administration, or equivalent

Experience

10 years practical experience in data processing environment and system programming

Special Training and Knowledge

Familiar with IBM, Tandem, and HP hardware

VM knowledge and expertise

Knowledge of CICS, VTAM, PC, VSAM, and teleprocessing or database software

Strong communication and writing skills

Appendix B5

PERSON SPECIFICATIONS FOR ASSISTANT COMPUTER PROGRAMMER

The Assistant Computer Programmer person specifications are accompanied by a job description. Both documents are "real," with company name excluded. Whereas the Manager sample had 38 person specifications, the less complex Assistant Computer Programmer person specs number only 20.

As with all of the sample person specifications, a similar job with identical job description might reasonably have some different person specs, with different base ratings, because of unique circumstances. The hiring manager, working with Human Resources, can best "tailor" the person specifications to define what it takes to do this particular job.

Scale: 4 = Excellent 2 = Only Fair 3 = Good 1 = Poor	Base Rating	Your Rating
1. *Analytic Skill:* Analyses problems in depth. Achieves satisfactory results on PAT and PI performance.	3	
2. *Judgment:* Demonstrates proficiency in at least one approved programming language or capacity to quickly develop it. Logical thinker. Shows "common sense." (4) level would represent current proficiency in more than one approved programming language, capacity for higher level decision making, or extraordinary ability to learn quickly.	3	

	Base Rating	Your Rating
3. *Oral Communications:* Exhibits ability to communicate thoughts clearly, avoiding "computer-ese," to users and to contribute to departmental or project status meetings.	2+	
4. *Written Communications:* Adequate ability to provide status reports, complete prescribed forms to change control, etc.	2	
5. *Education:* High school diploma. (3) would be Community College EDP diploma.	2	
6. *Experience:* One year programming. (3) would represent two or more years.	2	
7. *Self-Objectivity:* Demonstrates accurate self-insights, with respect to not just strengths, but also shortcomings and areas for improvement. Does not excessively rationalize or blame others for mistakes and failures.	3	
8. *Perseverance:* "Hangs in there" to successful completion, despite obstacles.	3	
9. *Independence:* Functions successfully without much supervision.	3	
10. *Standards of Performance:* Strives for and consistently achieves quality results; demonstrates low tolerance for mediocrity. Exhibits conscientiousness, dedication, self-discipline, and responsibility.	3	
11. *"Track Record":* Has successful career history. Repeated failures with "good excuses" probably not acceptable. Recent track record is weighed most heavily.	3	

	Base Rating	Your Rating
12. *Emotional Stability:* Under pressure from competition, time scarcity, personal problems, requirements by supervisors or other factors, retains emotional control, honesty, and productivity. Does not make "flighty" decisions or excessively "lose one's cool." Exhibits a positive self-concept. Able to "take rejection" while maintaining effectiveness.	3	
13. *Organization/Planning:* Accurately estimates time required to meet assignments. Is efficient and productive. Completes and submits Activity and Expense reports accurately and on time. (3) would represent project level organization/planning abilities.	2	
14. *First Impression:* Creates favorable first impression through acceptable attire, grooming, voice qualities, eye contact, gestures, personal hygiene, and bearing. Although (2) is acceptable initially, it is expected that the individual will have increasing client contact, so rapid progress toward (3) is necessary.	2+	
15. *Likability:* Wins liking and respect of people. Demonstrates flexibility, friendliness, and honesty in dealing with people.	3	
16. *Team Player:* Cooperates with supervisor; keeps supervisor informed on status of work. Cooperates with users (without being a "pushover"). Shows willingness and ability to assist in training trainee programmer. (4) would represent exceptional interpersonal skills.	3	
17. *Empathy/Listening:* "Tunes in" accurately to the feelings, needs, and attitudes of others; understands the impact of one's own behavior on others; demonstrates good listening skills.	3	

	Base Rating	Your Rating
18. *Motivation/Drive:* Exhibits strong desire to achieve, and an appropriately high dedication level. Although hours per se are less important than results, 40-45 hours or more per week are reasonably expected (particularly with increased client involvement). Must be willing to occasionally work odd hours in order to meet client needs.	3	
19. *Health:* Physical age equal to or less than chronological age. Maintains weight, diet, and alcohol use within normal range. Exercises regularly. Has no health problems that might seriously affect attendance or productivity.	3	
20. *Compatibility of Interests with the Company:* Demonstrates needs (for money, recognition, affiliation, achievement, prestige, promotion, power, location, amount and type of travel, or whatever) consistent with the opportunities available in the foreseeable future.	4	

JOB DESCRIPTION—ASSISTANT COMPUTER PROGRAMMER

Job Title: Assistant Computer Programmer

Reports to: Project Leader, Senior Programmer, or Analyst

Narrative Description

Working as a member of a project team, the junior programmer participates in the development and maintenance of computer-based business systems.

Responsibilities

1. Complete assignments according to specification and within allotted time.
2. Keep abreast of technical and environmental changes that may affect work.
3. Learn the standards and conventions in use for a particular department or client project.

4. Understand the basic knowledge of the Operating System pertinent to current assignment.
5. Develop proficiency in the use of at least one approved programming language.

Technical Duties

1. Code programs or changes from detailed specifications according to standards and conventions.
2. Prepare program and operations documentation according to standards.
3. Prepare test data.
4. Submit tests and verify results.
5. Prepare required JCL.
6. Participate in quality control procedures such as desk checking and structured walk-throughs.
7. Code and test utility programs such as sorts, file scans, etc.
8. Investigate and debug common program problems such as data and operations exceptions.
9. Compile programs and correct syntax and logic errors.
10. Act as on-call programmer for production systems. (This duty is normally assigned on a rotating basis, and the junior programmer will usually have a more senior programmer or supervisor available as back-up.)

Administrative Duties

1. Complete and submit Activity and Expense reports accurately and within prescribed time limits.
2. Attend departmental or project status meetings.
3. Provide written or verbal status reports on current assignments.
4. Assist in the orientation and training of trainee programmers.
5. Prepare estimates of time required to complete assignments.
6. When acting as on-call programmer, notify supervisor when the production problem cannot be resolved in the prescribed time period.
7. Complete and submit the prescribed forms for change control, library maintenance, etc.

Contacts Within Department

Senior Programmer or Analyst
Project Leader

Contacts Outside of Department

Operations

Client or User (rarely on development projects, but occasionally on maintenance projects)

PERSON SPECIFICATIONS FOR RETAIL SALES CLERK

The final set of sample person specifications is accompanied by a one-paragraph job description. The low base ratings are consistent with those for all jobs in the company. For example, throughout this company, Education base ratings are:

4 = Graduate degree (or equivalent)

3 = College degree (or equivalent)

2 = High school diploma (or equivalent)

1 = Grammar school diploma (or equivalent)

0 = Less than grammar school diploma

The base rating for education necessary for retail sales clerk is only 2, whereas for upper-level jobs, it is a 3 or higher.

Scale: 4 = Excellent 2 = Only Fair 3 = Good 1 = Poor	Base Rating	Your Rating
Intellectual Characteristics		
1. *Learning Ability:* Demonstrates ability and interest in learning about home improvement methods, products, and materials. This person specification reflects neither motivation to learn nor initiative.	2	
2. *Analytic Skill:* Quickly and correctly analyzes customer's project needs and skills.	3	
3. *Pragmatism:* Generates sensible, realistic, practical solutions to home improvement problems.	3	

	Base Rating	Your Rating

4. *Oral Communications:* Clear and concise in face-to-face communications. Need not use perfect grammar, but must communicate product features and give advice effectively. Must listen well and close sales. — **3**

5. *Education:* High school graduate or equivalent. — **2**

6. *Experience/Knowledge:* Must be knowledgeable (though not necessarily expert) in two or more departments and have two or more years of sales experience. — **2**

Personal Characteristics

7. *Motivation/Drive:* Exhibits energy and high dedication level. Forty hours or more per week are necessary, with constant walking and lifting. — **3**

8. *Initiative, a "Doer":* Actively seeks out opportunities to help customers. — **3**

9. *Organization/Planning:* Utilizes time effectively. Effectively juggles several customers' needs. Shows consistent reliability and self-discipline. History of no significant tardiness or absenteeism problems. — **2**

10. *Independence:* Functions successfully without much supervision. — **2**

11. *Emotional Stability:* Under pressure from multiple customers, occasional irate customers, hazardous actions by customers, shelves to be restocked, personal problems, requirements by supervisors, or other sources, retains emotional control, honesty, and productivity. Does not "lose one's cool." Exhibits a positive self-concept and generally positive outlook on life. — **3**

	Base Rating	Your Rating

12. *Self-Objectivity:* Recognizes not just one's own strengths, but also shortcomings and areas for improvement. Demonstrates the courage not to be defensive, rationalize mistakes, nor blame others for one's own failures. Builds feedback mechanisms to minimize "blind spots." — **3**

Note: High self-objectivity is necessary, but not sufficient for a person to be adaptable and self-correcting.

13. *Adaptability:* Converts high self-objectivity into self-correction and personal improvement. Actively supports necessary organization change. Not rigid—intellectually, emotionally, nor interpersonally. Adjusts quickly to changing priorities. — **2**

14. *Personal Integrity:* Remains consistently honest. — **3+**

Interpersonal Relations

15. *First Impression:* Creates favorable first impression through acceptable attire, body structure, grooming, voice qualities, eye contact, gestures, personal hygiene, and bearing. — **2+**

16. *Enthusiasm:* Exhibits positive attitude and excitement in helping meet customer's needs. — **3**

17. *Likability:* Wins the liking and respect of people. Demonstrates interpersonal flexibility, friendliness, sense of humor and genuineness. Exhibits warmth and caring. Shows tact and diplomacy. — **3**

18. *Empathy/Listening:* "Tunes in" accurately to the project needs, feelings, skills, and moods of customers. Understands the impact of one's behavior on others. Demonstrates good listening skills. — **3**

19. *Team Player:* Cooperates with supervisors and sales people in all departments. — **3**

	Base Rating	Your Rating

Additional Person Specifications

20. *Compatibility of Interests with Company:* Demonstrates needs (for money, recognition, affiliation, achievement, prestige, promotion, power, location, amount and type of travel, or whatever) consistent with the opportunities available in the foreseeable future. — Base Rating: **3**

21. *Health:* Has no health problems that might seriously affect attendance or productivity. Must be able to pass medical examination. — Base Rating: **3**

JOB DESCRIPTION—RETAIL SALES CLERK

(Retail Store—Home Improvement Center)

Responsibilities

Each sales clerk is assigned to one of eight departments. Walking the floor, the salesperson must greet customers, learn about the customer's home improvement projects, and offer practical suggestions for how to complete projects. Advises customers on location of products throughout the store. Helps customers move bulky, heavy loads safely through the store. Must remain calm, friendly, and helpful even in hectic peak periods. At slower periods, stocks merchandise, frequently lifting seventy-pound loads.

Application
Form

APPLICATION FORM/

You are not required to furnish any information which is prohibited by federal, state, or local law.

Last Name	First	Middle	Social Security No. ( )
Home Address	City	State	Zip Code	Area Code ( )	Telephone
Business Address	City	State	Zip Code	Area Code	Telephone

Position applied for_____Earnings Expected $_____

I. BUSINESS EXPERIENCE: (Please start with your present position.)

A. Firm_____Address_____ _____

City_____State_____Zip Code_____Phone ( )_____

Kind of Business _____Employed From_____To_____
(show months as well as years)

Title _____ Initial Compensation _____ Final Total Compensation _____ (Base _____ Bonus _____ Other _____)

Nature of Work_____
Supervisory Responsibility _____ Name & Title of Immediate Superior_____

What did you like most about your job?_____

Reasons for leaving or desiring to change_____

What did you least enjoy?_____

Reasons for leaving_____

B. Firm_____Address_____

City_____State_____Zip Code_____Phone ( )_____

Kind of Business_____Employed from_____To_____
(show months as well as years)

Title _____ Initial Compensation _____ Final Total Compensation _____ (Base _____ Bonus _____ Other _____)

Nature of Work_____
Supervisory Responsibility _____ Name & Title of Immediate Superior_____

What did you like most about your job?_____

Reasons for leaving or desiring to change_____

What did you least enjoy?_____

Reasons for leaving_____

C. Firm_____Address_____

City_____State_____Zip Code_____Phone (   )_____

Kind of Business_____Employed From_____To_____
(show months as well as years)

Title _____ Initial Compensation _____ Final Total Compensation _____ ⎛Base _____⎞
⎜Bonus _____⎟
⎝Other_____⎠

Nature of Work_____

Supervisory Responsibility _____ Name & Title of Immediate Superior _____

What did you like about your job?_____
_____

What did you least enjoy?_____
_____

Reasons for leaving_____
_____

Other Positions Held: a. Company b. City	a. Your Title b. Name of Superior	Date (mo./yr.) a. Began b. Left	Compensation a. Initial b. Final	a. Type of Work b. Reason for Leaving
D. a._____ b._____	a._____ b._____	a.__/___ b.__/___	a._____ b._____	a._____ b._____
E. _____ _____	_____ _____	___/___ ___/___	_____ _____	_____ _____
F. _____ _____	_____ _____	___/___ ___/___	_____ _____	_____ _____
G. _____ _____	_____ _____	___/___ ___/___	_____ _____	_____ _____

Indicate by letter_____any of the above employers you do **not** wish contacted.

II. MILITARY EXPERIENCE:

If in service, indicate: Branch_____Date (mo./yr.) entered_____Date (mo./yr.)discharged_____

Nature of duties_____

Highest rank or grade_____Terminal rank or grade_____

III. EDUCATION   Elementary 6 7 8   High School 1 2 3 4   College 1 2 3 4 5 6 7 8
(circle highest grade completed)

A. HIGH SCHOOL   Name of High School_____Location_____

Dates (mo./yr.) attended_____If graduated, month and year_____

Approximate number in graduating class_____Rank from top_____

Final grade point average_____(A = _____) Scores on SAT_____

Extracurricular activities_____

Offices, honors/awards _____

Part-time and summer work_____

B. COLLEGE/GRADUATE SCHOOL

Name & Location	From	To	Degree	Major	Grade Point Average	Total Credit Hours	Extracurricular Activities, Honors and Awards
					(A = ___)		
					(A = ___)		
					(A = ___)		

What undergraduate courses did you like most_____Why_____

What undergraduate courses did you like least_____Why_____

How was your education financed_____

Part-time and summer work_____

Other courses, seminars, or studies_____

IV. PHYSICAL DATA:

Condition of Health:_____
Date of most recent physical exam_____

What physical limitations do you have that might have a direct bearing on job performance?_____

List any serious illnesses, operations, accidents or nervous disorders you may have had with approximate dates

V. ACTIVITIES:

Membership in professional or job-relevant organizations. (You may exclude racial, religious and nationality groups)

Publications, patents, inventions, professional licenses or special honors or awards_____

What qualifications, abilities, and strong points will help you succeed in this job?_____

What are your shortcomings and areas for improvement?_____

VI. AIMS:

What income would you need (in today's dollar value) in order to live the way you would like to live? (Your response will not be taken as dissatisfaction with your present salary, but refers to the salary which you ultimately wish to attain.)

_____

Willing to relocate? Yes_____ No_____ Any restrictions_____

Amount of overnight travel acceptable_____

_____

What are your plans for the future_____

_____

_____

_____

_____

_____

_____

_____

_____

_____

VII. OTHER:

Are you a U.S. citizen? Yes ☐   No ☐

If any personal, financial, or family circumstances might conceivably have bearing on any aspect of job performance, explain

in full_____

_____

_____

Have you ever been convicted of a felony? Yes ☐   No ☐

If so, explain_____

_____

_____

I authorize all schools, credit bureaus and law enforcement agencies to supply information concerning my background. I understand that I have a right to request disclosure of the nature, scope, and results of such an inquiry. I understand that if any statement herein is not true, an offer of employment may be withdrawn.

_____
Signature

_____
Date

smart & associates, inc.

CIVIC OPERA BUILDING • 20 NORTH WACKER DRIVE
CHICAGO, ILLINOIS 60606 • 312-726-7820

In-Depth Reference Check Guide

In-Depth
REFERENCE CHECK
GUIDE

Bradford D. Smart, Ph.D.

Reference check conducted by _____

Name of Applicant (A)_____ Date _____

Home Phone _____

Office Phone_____

Individual Contacted _____ Title _____

Company Name _____

General Principles

- In-depth reference checks should be conducted by the **hiring manager.** (Human resources should conduct preliminary reference checks, early in the selection process, simply to verify dates of employment and job title).

- In-depth reference checks should be performed **after** the in-depth selection interview.

- Contact previous **supervisors,** particularly those the applicant (A) has reported to during the past five years.

- Obtain **written permission** from (A) to conduct reference checks.

- Do not call those listed as "references" in a resume ... unless the list contains a recent supervisor's name.

- During the in-depth selection interview ask the applicant the name, title and location of each supervisor. Then ask (A) "would you please contact (the previous supervisor) **at home,** and ask if she would accept a telephone call from me at home sometime soon?"

- Promise those contacted total **confidentiality,** and honor that promise.

- Contact the person **at home,** preferably on the weekend.

- Create the tone in which you are a trusted colleague ... a fellow professional who knows (A) very well, who just might hire (A) and who is apt to better manage (A) if (person contacted) will be kind enough to share some insights.

- Contact the **current** supervisor. If this is not acceptable to (A) until a written offer is formally accepted, make it clear that a job offer will be **contingent upon "no surprises"** in reference checks that **will be** performed at a mutually agreed upon time.

Note: A coin toss resulted in the decision to refer to Applicant (A) as "he" and the supervisor contacted as "she".

Introductory Comments

"Hello, (name of person contacted), thank you very much for (returning/accepting) my call. As (A) indicated, we are considering hiring him and I would **very much** appreciate your comments on his strengths, areas for improvement and how I might best manage him. Could I impose on you for a few minutes to get your insights -- it would be very helpful to (A) and me. And, of course, anything you tell me will be held in the strictest confidence." (Assuming concurrence ...) "Great, thank you very much. (A) and I have spent _____ hours together... I have thoroughly reviewed his career history and plans for the future and I was particularly interested in his experiences when he reported to you. If you don't mind, why don't we start with a very general question ..."

Comprehensive Appraisal

"What would you consider (A)'s:

Strengths, Assets, Things You Like and Respect About Him, Personally and Professionally, and His ...	Shortcomings, Weaker Points, and Areas For Improvement?"

Notes:

- It is OK to interrupt strengths to get clarification, but do not do so for shortcomings. Get the longest list of shortcomings possible and then go back for clarification. If you interrupt the negatives and get elaboration, the tone might seem too negative, thus closing off discussion of further negatives.

- If you are getting a "white wash," inquire about negatives directly. For example: "John said that he missed the software project due date by three months and guesses that that hurt his overall performance rating. Could you elaborate?"

Responsibilities/Accountabilities

"Would you please clarify what (A)'s responsibilities and accountabilities were in that position?"

_____

_____

_____

Overall Performance Rating

"On a scale of excellent, good, fair or poor, how would you rate (A)'s overall performance?

_____

Why? _____

Is (A) eligible for re-hire?" _____

Confirmation of Dates/Compensation

"Just to clean up a couple of details, what were (A)'s starting _____
and final _____ employment dates? What were his initial _____
and final _____ compensation levels?"

Description of Position Applied For

"Let me tell you more about the job (A) is applying for." (Describe the job)

Good/Bad Fit

"Now, how do you think (A) might fit in that job?" (Probe for specifics)

Good Fit Indicators	Bad Fit Indicators

Comprehensive Ratings

"Now that I've described the job that (A) is applying for and you've told me quite a bit about his strengths and shortcomings, would you please rate him on nine categories? An excellent, good, fair, and poor scale would be fine."

	Rating	Comments *
1. Thinking skills ... judgement, analytic ability, pragmatism, decisiveness, creativity, ability to juggle several projects simultaneously		
2. Communications ... one-one, in meetings, speeches, and written communications		
3. Technical skills/experience/ education		
4. Initiative, perseverance, independence, high standards of performance		
5. Emotional stability and maturity, willingness to admit mistakes and absence of personal problems that might interfere with the job		
6. Work habits ... time management, organization and planning		
7. People skills ... first impression made, ability to win the liking and respect of people, assertiveness, cooperativeness, willingness to take direction, enthusiasm and empathy		
8. Motivation/drive/ambition/health		
9. Managerial abilities ... leadership, ability to hire the best people, ability to train and develop people, willingness to fire those who are hopelessly incompetent, delegation, monitoring performance and creating team efforts		

* **Note:** Probe for specifics. Don't accept vague generalities ("he sometimes procrastinates") but ask for concrete examples, dates, consequences, etc.

Questions for Me as Hiring Manager
"What would be your best advice to me for how I could best manage (A)?"

_____
_____
_____
_____
_____
_____

Final Comments
"Have you any final comments or suggestions about (A)?"

_____
_____
_____
_____
_____
_____

Thanks!
"I would like to thank you very much for your insightful and useful comments and suggestions. Before we close, please let me know which of your comments I can share with others and which should be just between the two of us."

_____
_____
_____
_____
_____
_____

smart & associates, inc.

CIVIC OPERA BUILDING • 20 NORTH WACKER DRIVE
CHICAGO, ILLINOIS 60606 • 312-726-7820

Professional Rapport Rating Form

PROFESSIONAL RAPPORT RATING FORM

Interviewer _____ Interviewee _____

Observer _____ Date _____

Number of Minutes Observed _____

Rating scale: 4 = Excellent, 3 = Good, 2 = Needs Improvement, 1 = Good Grief,
               N/A = Not observed *and* would not have been appropriate or useful in interview.

INITIAL RAPPORT BUILDING   RATING

1. *Greeting* (warm, friendly, smile, handshake)   _____

   Comments: _____

2. Offered something to *drink*   _____

   Comments: _____

3. *"Idle chit chat"* (couple of minutes—enough to get interviewee talking comfortably)   _____

   Comments: _____

4. Stated *purposes* and expected *timing*   _____

   Comments: _____

5. *Mechanics* (appropriate seating, all forms handy, notebook used, private location)   _____

   Comments: _____

THROUGHOUT THE INTERVIEW

1. *All appropriate questions* in Interview Guide asked without harmfully altering the wording
   Open-ended (not yes/no) questions favored   _____

   Comments: _____

2. Interviewer *"connecting"* with interviewee on human level   _____

   Comments: _____

Rating scale: 4 = Excellent, 3 = Good, 2 = Needs Improvement, 1 = Good Grief,
                N/A = Not observed *and* would not have been appropriate or useful in interview.

RATING

3. *Eye contact* (minimum of 20%, but no staring)   _____

   Comments: _____

4. *Friendliness,* warmth   _____

   Comments: _____

5. *Enthusiasm*   _____

   Comments: _____

6. *Control* maintained   _____

   Comments: _____

7. *Humor*   _____

   Comments: _____

8. Appears *sincere*   _____

   Comments: _____

9. *Thorough* note-taking on content and context (determined after interview)   _____

   Comments: _____

10. *Unobstrusive* note-taking   _____

    Comments: _____

11. *Follow-up questions* asked, with appropriate wording and style, and specific meanings determined   _____
    for vague responses

    Comments: _____

12. *Absence of* (unintended) *biasing* of question responses   _____

    Comments: _____

13. *Interviewee talks 90%* (4), 80%, (3), 70% (2), less than 70% (1)   _____

    Comments: _____

14. Appropriate *vocabulary* level   _____

    Comments: _____

15. Voice *clarity*   _____

    Comments: _____

Rating scale: 4 = Excellent, 3 = Good, 2 = Needs Improvement, 1 = Good Grief,
N/A = Not observed *and* would not have been appropriate or useful in interview.

RATING

16. Vocal *range* (not monotone) _____

Comments: _____

17. *Expressiveness:* (interested, friendly, half-smile; not blank, not excessive frowning) _____

Comments: _____

18. Interview *pace* (neither too fast nor too slow) _____

Comments: _____

19. Use of *applicant's name* (once every 5-10 minutes) _____

Comments: _____

20. *Show of approval* of openness or when interviewee is obviously proud of an unambiguous accomplishment _____

Comments: _____

21. *Protection of interviewee's ego* (use of "weasel words" rather than unintended bluntness) _____

Comments: _____

22. *Control* of shock, dismay, surprise, anger _____

Comments: _____

23. *Breaks* (every 45 minutes) _____

Comments: _____

24. Consistently shows *respect* for interviewee _____

Comments: _____

INTERVIEW PROBES

1. Thorough *summary* (at least one every 10-15 minutes) _____

Comments: _____

2. Pregnant *pause* _____

Comments: _____

3. *Affirmation* of understanding ("I see," "uh hu," a nod, etc.) _____

Comments: _____

Rating scale: 4 = Excellent, 3 = Good, 2 = Needs Improvement, 1 = Good Grief,
            N/A = Not observed *and* would not have been appropriate or useful in interview.

RATING

4. *Echo* (repeating all or part of a response)   _____

   Comments: _____

5. *Active listening* (reflecting interviewee's unstated feelings) so as to deepen understanding and profes-   _____
   sional rapport

   Comments: _____

6. *Direct question* (usually used when softer approaches have failed)   _____

   Comments: _____

7. *TORC* Methods   _____

   Comments: _____

SUMMARY

Overall level of Professional Rapport achieved

              4 _____

            3.5 _____

              3 _____

            2.5 _____

              2 _____

            1.5 _____

              1 _____

             .5 _____

Index